From PHP to Ruby on Rails

Transition from PHP to Ruby by leveraging your existing backend programming knowledge

Bernard Pineda

BIRMINGHAM—MUMBAI

From PHP to Ruby on Rails

Group Product Manager: Rohit Rajkumar

Publishing Product Manager: Himani Dewan

Book Project Manager: Aishwarya Mohan

Senior Editor: Rakhi Patel

Technical Editor: Simran Udasi

Copy Editor: Safis Editing

Proofreader: Safis Editing

Indexer: Rekha Nair

Production Designer: Jyoti Kadam

DevRel Marketing Coordinators: Namita Velgekar and Nivedita Pandey

First published: December 2023

Production reference: 1161123

Published by Packt Publishing Ltd.
Grosvenor House
11 St Paul's Square
Birmingham
B3 1RB, UK

ISBN 978-1-80461-009-1

www.packtpub.com

To my brother Benjamin, who in spite of all that he's been through keeps on smiling, shining, and thriving.

– Bernardo Pineda

Contributors

About the author

Bernard Pineda has been working in the IT industry since 2002. He worked as a PHP and Ruby on Rails developer for many years, mostly as a freelance developer. He is also a LinkedIn Learning instructor with many courses in both Spanish and English. He has also participated as a speaker on a round table at Campus Party 2010 discussing PHP frameworks. He has written articles regarding Angular and Adobe's Flex platform. He has worked with different technologies throughout his career, including PHP, Ruby, Java, Python, and Angular, and considers himself a language-agnostic developer. He is currently a site reliability engineer working in the Bay Area. In his spare time, he plays and records music, and also writes screenplays for fun.

I want to thank my wife, Gaby, for all her support during the good times and the bad. She has been the best partner and teammate I could have ever asked for and played a crucial role for me to be able to succeed in this endeavor. I would also like to thank my close friends, who have always pushed me to follow my dreams. Thank you all.

About the reviewers

Ali Onuche John is a distinguished global senior data scientist and enterprise software developer with over 16 years of experience in spearheading the development of ERP software applications across various industries. He also holds the position of CEO at Code Factory, a prominent software development company. Ali's illustrious career epitomizes a remarkable blend of theoretical expertise and practical finesse, solidifying his status as a maestro at the crossroads of machine learning and software development. Recognized as a thought leader in this field, Ali has left an indelible mark through his notable contributions in the form of publications and workshops. His steadfast dedication to pushing the boundaries of technology is unmistakable, and his perpetual presence at the vanguard of the industry underscores his significant influence in shaping the continually evolving landscape of machine learning and software development. Moreover, Ali brings his valuable experience in the field of climate change, further diversifying his impressive portfolio of expertise and contributions to address critical global challenges.

Melashu Amare is an experienced full stack software engineer who specializes in Ruby, Ruby on Rails, PostgreSQL, Redis, Hotwire, TailwindCSS, RSpec, and Sidekiq. He has contributed to several open source projects and built his own gems. He has also worked as a coding instructor for a few years and has gained extensive experience in mentoring other developers. Before diving into full stack web development, he worked as a mobile application developer using the hybrid mobile application framework Flutter, as well as PHP and MySQL.

Omar Alvarado Luna, a "code investor," aids businesses in managing code debt through best practices and research. With expertise in PHP, Node.js, Ruby, Bash, and Python, he's an advocate for cultural and technical best practices. Currently making an impact in the finance and banking sector, his insights enhanced this book. Omar champions methods that drive high-performance teams.

Table of Contents

3

Comparing Basic Ruby Syntax to PHP   31

4

Ruby Scripting versus PHP Scripting   61

5

Libraries and Class Syntax   87

6

Debugging Ruby   105

Part 2: Ruby and the Web

7

Understanding Convention over Configuration   127

8

Models, DBs, and Active Record   153

9

Bringing It All Together   173

10

Considerations for Hosting Rails Applications versus PHP Applications   203

Index   217

Preface

Hi, all! *From PHP to Ruby to Rails* is a guide for people who have a PHP background and understanding but wish to extend their knowledge to another object-oriented programming language: Ruby. Ruby is a programming language originally created by Yukihiro "Matz" Matsumoto and publicly released in 1995. Since its inception, Ruby has been a very verbose language, and the open source community has adopted this trait to make Ruby programs very explicit regarding the intent of each line of code. This guide will not only teach you Ruby's language features but also help you get into the mindset of Ruby application development. Along this journey of learning Ruby, you will also learn the basics of Ruby on Rails, a framework for creating web applications developed by David Heinemeier Hansson and released as an open source tool in 2004. With the growing popularity and adoption of Ruby and Ruby on Rails by tech companies, there is a lot of demand for Ruby developers all over the world. Whether you're curious about Ruby and Ruby on Rails or want to find out whether Ruby is for you, this guide is for you.

Who this book is for

This book is for people who already have some programming experience and wish to take advantage of that experience and knowledge to learn the Ruby programming language and mindset.

The three types of people who will benefit the most from this book are the following:

- Developers who have worked with another programming language.

- Developers who have had experience working with PHP and would like to learn another programming language. They will gain knowledge of the Ruby language through examples and examinations of equivalent PHP code.

- Developers who have experience of working with any PHP framework (Laravel, CodeIgniter, Symfony, CakePHP, etc.). The book covers the Ruby on Rails framework. People familiar with any web framework will benefit from learning the **Model-View-Controller** (**MVC**) implementation of Ruby on Rails.

What this book covers

Chapter 1, *Understanding the Ruby Mindset and Culture*, provides an introduction to the way Ruby developers think and write code.

Chapter 2, *Setting Up Our Local Environment*, provides a short guide to installing Ruby to allow you to follow along with the exercises in this book.

Chapter 3, Comparing Basic Ruby Syntax to PHP, provides a comparison between PHP and Ruby syntax as a way to ease your entry into the language, its similarities, and its differences.

Chapter 4, Ruby Scripting versus PHP Scripting, compares PHP scripts with Ruby scripts with the intent of taking advantage of Ruby's syntax to write more readable code.

Chapter 5, Libraries and Class Syntax, provides an introduction to Ruby's libraries (gems) and their installation and usage. This chapter also provides an introduction to object-oriented programming in the Ruby realm.

Chapter 6, Debugging Ruby, provides an introduction to the tools we have available in Ruby to fix bugs and errors in scripts that we may encounter at runtime. This chapter also provides a guide to installing and using these tools.

Chapter 7, Understanding Convention over Configuration, provides an introduction to the Ruby on Rails web framework, its installation, and the simplest of examples to start using it.

Chapter 8, Models, DBs, and Active Record, provides an introduction to handling databases with Ruby on Rails through models. It also covers the basics of database actions using `ActiveRecord`.

Chapter 9, Bringing It All Together, provides a guide to generate a simple Ruby on Rails application using everything we've learned so far in the book, but via a more practical example.

Chapter 10, Considerations for Hosting Rails Applications versus PHP Applications, provides a short guide to the factors that you must take into account when publishing a Rails application in a real-life scenario, a.k.a. production.

To get the most out of this book

You will need Ruby 3.1.1 installed (follow the instructions in the book if needed to set up Ruby). You will also need Git installed on your computer as Ruby libraries (gems) rely on git to obtain its source code. If you're using macOS, you will require either Xcode command-line tools or Xcode itself to be installed before you can use Ruby. Though not compulsory, you should also install `rbenv` to allow yourself to install different versions of Ruby.

Software/hardware covered in the book	Operating system requirements
Ruby	Windows, macOS, or Linux
Ruby on Rails	Windows, macOS, or Linux

Linux users will have to install a selection of libraries with the following command (or its equivalent as appropriate for the distribution you use):

```
sudo yum install git-core zlib zlib-devel gcc-c++ patch readline
readline-devel libyaml-devel libffi-devel openssl-devel make bzip2
autoconf automake libtool bison curl sqlite-devel
```

If you are using the digital version of this book, we advise you to type the code yourself or access the code from the book's GitHub repository (a link is available in the next section). Doing so will help you avoid any potential errors related to the copying and pasting of code.

Download the example code files

You can download the example code files for this book from GitHub at `https://github.com/PacktPublishing/From-PHP-to-Ruby-on-Rails`. If there's an update to the code, it will be updated in the GitHub repository.

We also have other code bundles from our rich catalog of books and videos available at `https://github.com/PacktPublishing/`. Check them out!

Conventions used

There are a number of text conventions used throughout this book.

`Code in text`: Indicates code words in text, database table names, folder names, filenames, file extensions, pathnames, dummy URLs, user input, and Twitter handles. Here is an example: "In Ruby, we don't really have a `var_dump()` function, but instead every object has a method already available called `inspect()`."

A block of code is set as follows:

```
require 'oj'
json_text = '{"name":"Sarah Kerrigan", "age":23, "human":true}'
ruby_hash = Oj.load(json_text)
puts ruby_hash
puts ruby_hash["name"]
```

Any command-line input or output is written as follows:

```
gem uninstall oj
```

Bold: Indicates a new term, an important word, or words that you see onscreen. For instance, words in menus or dialog boxes appear in **bold**. Here is an example: "And when you click on the **Sign up** button, you should immediately see the page you were trying to browse to before being redirected."

> Tips or important notes
> Appear like this.

Get in touch

Feedback from our readers is always welcome.

General feedback: If you have questions about any aspect of this book, email us at `customercare@packtpub.com` and mention the book title in the subject of your message.

Errata: Although we have taken every care to ensure the accuracy of our content, mistakes do happen. If you have found a mistake in this book, we would be grateful if you would report this to us. Please visit `www.packtpub.com/support/errata` and fill in the form.

Piracy: If you come across any illegal copies of our works in any form on the internet, we would be grateful if you would provide us with the location address or website name. Please contact us at `copyright@packtpub.com` with a link to the material.

If you are interested in becoming an author: If there is a topic that you have expertise in and you are interested in either writing or contributing to a book, please visit `authors.packtpub.com`.

Share Your Thoughts

Once you've read *From PHP to Ruby on Rails*, we'd love to hear your thoughts! Scan the QR code below to go straight to the Amazon review page for this book and share your feedback.

`https://packt.link/r/1804610097`

Your review is important to us and the tech community and will help us make sure we're delivering excellent quality content.

Download a free PDF copy of this book

Thanks for purchasing this book!

Do you like to read on the go but are unable to carry your print books everywhere?

Is your eBook purchase not compatible with the device of your choice?

Don't worry, now with every Packt book you get a DRM-free PDF version of that book at no cost.

Read anywhere, any place, on any device. Search, copy, and paste code from your favorite technical books directly into your application.

The perks don't stop there, you can get exclusive access to discounts, newsletters, and great free content in your inbox daily

Follow these simple steps to get the benefits:

1. Scan the QR code or visit the link below

https://packt.link/free-ebook/9781804610091

2. Submit your proof of purchase

3. That's it! We'll send your free PDF and other benefits to your email directly

Part 1:
From PHP to
Ruby Basics

In this part, you will be introduced to the whole Ruby way of doing things while comparing it to the way you would do those things with PHP. In addition to this, you will also learn how to use what Ruby brings to the table in terms of syntax, libraries (called gems), and debugging tools to make troubleshooting as painless as possible.

This part has the following chapters:

- *Chapter 1, Understanding the Ruby Mindset and Culture*
- *Chapter 2, Setting Up Our Local Environment*
- *Chapter 3, Comparing Basic Ruby Syntax to PHP*
- *Chapter 4, Ruby Scripting versus PHP Scripting*
- *Chapter 5, Libraries and Class Syntax*
- *Chapter 6, Debugging Ruby*

1
Understanding the Ruby Mindset and Culture

Ruby has had quite a history since its inception by Yukihiro Matsumoto. The adoption of the language by the community has, of course, influenced the direction in which Ruby has been focused. But, at its core, Ruby has been very straightforward in the way you *can* and the way you *should* write programs/scripts with it. Every language has its own peculiarities, which the community takes to define what a good practice is and what is considered "bad" code. While this may be entirely subjective, this subjectiveness paves the way for what the author's original intention for creating the language was into what the community wants the language to become.

Ruby was created with the idea of being extremely easy to read, flexible, and object-oriented. The same can be said about the technologies that came to pass because of Ruby. I'm talking about frameworks created in Ruby, such as Ruby on Rails (`https://rubyonrails.org`) and Sinatra (`http://sinatrarb.com/`). But I'm also talking about other tools that were created with that same mindset, such as Chef (`https://www.chef.io/`). All of these tools have common traits but the trait that stands out the most is readability. Once you're in the Ruby "realm," you're able to read and understand code made for vanilla Ruby, a Ruby on Rails application API, or even a Chef recipe to manage and configure infrastructure. Ruby does not automatically make your code more understandable or readable, but it goes a long way to give you the tools to make your code easier to read. Making your code understandable is key to focusing more on the business (or hobby) at hand and focusing less on trying to understand what some code is doing.

But before we get there, we will need to make the switch to the Ruby mindset. In this chapter, we will start our journey into this mindset by covering the following topics:

- Creating readable Ruby code
- Object-oriented Ruby
- Writing Ruby-esque code

You made up your mind to learn a new programming language. Congratulations! I, for one, would like to applaud this decision and hope it took you less time than it took me to be seriously curious about another programming language. I was a bit stubborn and reluctant at first, seeing every single downside of Ruby. My favorite phrase was, "I can do that in PHP easier." But then, one day, it simply clicked and I never went back. Ruby has been my go-to language for a long time now. And I won´t try to oversell this to you. I refuse to say that Ruby is the best programming language there is because that would be answering a loaded question. There is no programming language that is universally better than the rest. What I can do is try to show you why I love Ruby.

Technical requirements

To follow along with this book, you will need:

- Git client

- rbenv (Ruby version manager to enable multiple versions of Ruby)

- Ruby (versions 2.6.10 and 3.0 or above)

- Any IDE of your choice installed to edit code (Sublime, Visual Studio Code, vim, Emacs, Rubymine, etc.)

All code examples have been written to work with Ruby versions 2.6.10 and 3.0 (or above). Some of the examples will need previous versions of Ruby (i.e. 2.6.10) to work with previous versions of Ruby on Rails (e.g. Ruby on Rails 5), but to guarantee that they work the same way as in this chapter, you should try to install the latest version of Ruby. You may get the installer for different operating systems here: `https://www.ruby-lang.org/en/downloads/`.

Additionally, to be able to use different versions of Ruby, I would also suggest you install rbenv from this GitHub repository: `https://github.com/rbenv/rbenv`.

The code presented in this book is available at `https://github.com/PacktPublishing/From-PHP-to-Ruby-on-Rails`.

Ruby is meant to be read as sentences

Having said all that about Ruby, let's get our hands dirty and start with the most basic of concepts. You already know about PHP variables. Variables hold information that can be used and referenced in our program. Also, PHP is a dynamically typed language, which means that the PHP "engine," which interprets our PHP code, will automatically infer the type of content within that variable. That's to say the following two things:

- We don't have to define what type of content our variable has

- A variable can change types without failing

Coming from PHP, you won't have to break your head to learn a new way of using or defining variables with Ruby, as Ruby behaves exactly the same way. However, beware that in other languages that are strongly typed, such as Java, a variable has to be defined with the type that it will contain and it can't change types over time.

So let's play around with some variables in PHP:

```
<?php
$name = "bernard";
$age = 40;
$height_in_cms = 177.5;
$chocolate_allergy = true;
$travel_bucket_list = ["Turkey", "Japan", "Canada"];
```

Ruby is not much different in this scenario:

```
name = "bernard";
age = 40;
height_in_cms = 177.5;
chocolate_allergy = true;
travel_bucket_list = ["Turkey", "Japan", "Canada"];
```

For those experienced PHP developers reading this whose eyes might be bleeding from my lack of using **PHP Standard Recommendation (PSR)** standards on the PHP block, I apologize, but I wanted to give you a glimpse of how the code could be written in a similar manner rather than focusing on PHP's best practices. Notice that we just wrote the variable names without the $ symbol. Another difference between PHP and Ruby is that we do not use any tag to denote PHP code, whereas, in PHP, we use the opening PHP tags (<?php). So, the main differences (so far) between our snippets are the way we call PHP code with the PHP tags and the way we refer to variables. While this is a functioning Ruby code, I intentionally wrote the Ruby block very PHP-esque to also give you all a glimpse of Ruby's flexibility. Ruby is extremely flexible to the point of being able to bend Ruby's own behavior. An example of this flexibility is that while we can add a semicolon (;) at the end of each line, it is a Ruby best practice to leave them out. Should this topic of Ruby's flexibility interest you, you may want to check metaprogramming in Ruby. This Ruby guide is a great starting point:

```
https://www.rubyguides.com/2016/04/metaprogramming-in-the-wild/
```

But let's not get ahead of ourselves, as this topic is really a complex one – at least for a beginner Ruby programmer.

Given the preceding code in PHP, let´s now determine whether the name is empty. In PHP, you would use the empty internal function. We surround it with another internal function called var_dump to show the contents of the empty function result:

```
$name = "Bernard";
var_dump( empty($name) );
```

This will output the following:

```
bool(false)
```

According to the documentation of the `empty` function, this is `false` because the name is not an empty string. Now, let's try that in Ruby:

```
name = "bernard";
puts name.empty?;
```

There are a couple of things that we have to notice here. The first thing that comes to mind is that this is read almost as a sentence. This is one of the key points to how the Ruby community has come together and used Ruby to make code that is read by humans. For the most part, you should avoid writing comments on your code unless it's for copyright and/or it does require an explanation. Ruby goes as far as having a strange way to write multiline comments. If I were to write a multiline comment on my code, I would have to look the syntax up because I've never used that notation. That's not to say that you can't or that you shouldn't. It's there for a reason. It simply means that the Ruby community seldom uses that notation. To write a comment in Ruby, you would simply add the hashtag symbol (#) as the first character on a line:

```
# This is a comment
```

As you know from comments within a snippet of code, this line will be ignored by Ruby. Keep in mind that a programming language, just like a spoken language, evolves due to its use. The best of tools may be lost just because no one uses them. Part of learning a language also involves learning the usage of the tools and best practices. This includes knowing what the Ruby community has decided not to exploit and what to use. So, while the community rarely uses multiline comments, all Ruby developers will take advantage of one of its most powerful tools: objects.

Everything is an object

The second thing that came to my mind while reading the previous code is that we are calling a method on a string. Now, let's step back a bit, and this is where we start looking at code through our newbie set of Ruby eyes. Our variable name contains a string. Does this mean that our name is an object? Well, the short answer is *Yes*. Almost everything in Ruby is an object. I know this might seem as if we're skipping a few chapters, but bear with me. We will see Ruby's object-oriented syntax in *Chapter 5*. For now, let's take this a step further within our code by getting what type of object our variable has with the following line:

```
puts name.class();
```

This will return the type of class of our object (in this specific case, `String`). We are able to do the same with the rest of our variables and we would get similar values (`Integer`, `Float`, `TrueClass`, or `Array`). And to take this even further to prove my point that almost everything in Ruby is an object, let's read the following example:

```
puts "benjamin".class();
```

This will also return a `String` type. So, bear that in mind when you're writing Ruby code. Now, let's go back to the initial example with the `empty` function:

```
name = "bernard";
puts name.empty?();
```

The third thing we also notice is that we are actually asking a question. This baffled me the first time I saw it. How do you know when to ask? Is Ruby *so* intuitive that you can actually ask questions? What type of sorcery is this? Unfortunately, the truth is far less ominous than the code itself. In Ruby, we can name a function or a method with the question mark symbol as part of the name, solely to improve readability. It does not have any special execution or meaning to the Ruby interpreter. We are just able to name a method/function like that. Having said that, by convention, Ruby developers use the question mark to hint that we will return a Boolean value. In this case, it merely answers the question about the emptiness of the variable name. Simply put, if the name is empty, the question will return a `true` value, and vice versa. This naming technique is part of the Ruby philosophy to make our whole code readable. Additionally, this type of code style is permeated throughout many of Ruby's internal classes. Some methods that are attached to number objects and array objects are an example of this. Here are a few examples:

- `.odd?`
- `.even?`
- `.include?`

All these examples were named like that for the sole purpose of readability and nothing more. Some of them are even shared between different classes but have their own implementation for each type. While we are currently looking at the question mark symbol, let's take a peek at a similar symbol: the exclamation point (`!`). Also known as a bang, it has a slightly different connotation within Ruby developers. Let's look at it with an example.

Let's show the name in uppercase letters. In PHP, we would write the following:

```
$name = "bernard";
echo strtoupper($name);
```

In Ruby, the same can be accomplished with the following code:

```
name = "bernard";
puts(name.upcase());
```

In both cases, this will return the name in uppercase (BERNARD). However, if we make any additional references to the name variable, the variable will remain unchanged:

```
name = "bernard";
puts(name.upcase());
puts(name);
```

This would return the following:

```
BERNARD
bernard
```

But what happens if we add the bang symbol (!)?

```
name = "bernard";
puts(name.upcase!());
puts(name);
```

This will return the name in uppercase twice:

```
BERNARD
BERNARD
```

The bang symbol in fact modifies the variable contents permanently. Functions that are named with the bang symbol are referred to as **destructive methods** because they modify or mutate the original object rather than just return the modified value. Examples of this are these methods from the `String` and `Array` classes:

- `.downcase!`
- `.reverse!`
- `.strip!`
- `.flatten!`

We can infer what they do just from reading them, but we now know what the bang symbol means in this context. Be careful when using these, but also don't be shy of using them when the use case requires it. Now, when you read Ruby code, you will be aware of the question mark (?) and the bang (!) symbol.

Transitioning to Ruby

So far, we've seen examples in which our code looks very similar to PHP. As I mentioned before, I purposely did this to showcase the flexibility of Ruby. This makes the change to Ruby easier than other languages in which the syntax is a lot different than Ruby. However, this is only the beginning of our journey to becoming a Ruby developer. If we want to be able to read and write Ruby code and snippets like seasoned Ruby developers, we will need to see how the community has come to make Ruby code. In short, while we can write our code similar to other languages, we should avoid this practice and, in the process, learn about what Ruby has to offer to make our code more and more readable.

The first step we are going to take toward this goal is to remove unnecessary syntax within our code. To do this, we also must understand the utility of what we are removing.

Let's take for an example our original code:

```
name = "bernard";
age = 40;
height_in_cms = 177.5;
chocolate_allergy = true;
travel_bucket_list = ["Turkey", "Japan", "Canada"];
```

In Ruby, the semicolon can be useful to separate multiline code into a single line dividing each line with a semicolon. If we took the name and the example to turn it into uppercase, we would have the following:

```
name = "bernard"; name.upcase!(); puts(name);
```

And this works perfectly fine. But remember, we are trying to make our code more readable. This is not more readable. It's the opposite. And, if we are not going to write our whole code in a single line, then let's take the original snippet (in multiple lines), and remove every single semicolon. This is starting to look more like Ruby:

```
name = "bernard"
age = 40
height_in_cms = 177.5
chocolate_allergy = true
travel_bucket_list = ["Turkey", "Japan", "Canada"]
```

This certainly seems to improve readability slightly by removing unused characters, but we are not finished. Let's put this into practice with another example. Let's write an example that will print out the string `This person is allergic to chocolate` if the value of the `$chocolate_allergy` variable is set to `true`. Because of our background in PHP, we might be compelled to write something similar to PHP. In PHP, we would write the following:

```
$chocolate_allergy = true;
if($chocolate_ allergy)
{
  echo "This person is allergic to chocolate";
}
```

With this in mind, we would write the following in Ruby:

```
chocolate_allergy = true
if(chocolate_allergy)
  puts("This person is allergic to chocolate")
end
```

This works fine, but it still looks a lot like PHP. An intermediate Ruby developer would most likely write something like this:

```
chocolate_allergy = true
puts "This person is allergic to chocolate"
  if chocolate_allergy
```

This is getting more and more readable by the second. But it also brings a couple of new practices to the table. For starters, the `puts` sentence is not surrounded by parenthesis. This is because, in Ruby, the use of parenthesis is optional for functions and methods. This is extremely useful as it's starting to read like plain English. It works with functions with multiple arguments, too. As an example, an implemented function could very well look like this:

```
add_locations "location 1", "location 2"
```

Of course, this becomes cumbersome if we need to call nested functions. Let's take this example with two functions:

```
def concatenate( text1, text2 )
  puts text1 + " " + text2
end
def to_upper( text )
  return text.upcase()
end
```

The `concatenate` function takes two strings and prints out both strings joined with a space between them. The second function just turns the input string into an uppercase string and returns the value. And this is where it could become problematic if we failed to use the parenthesis. If we wanted to concatenate the two strings and turn each string into an uppercase string, we could try the following:

```
concatenate to_upper "something", to_upper "else"
```

But we would fail miserably because the Ruby interpreter doesn't know that `"something"` is the argument for the `to_upper` function. We can easily fix this with parenthesis:

```
concatenate to_upper("something"), to_upper("else")
```

Be careful with this knowledge as, like everything else, if overdone, it can be detrimental to our code's readability. There are two additional points that we need to consider while deciding whether to use parenthesis. The first is that these rules also apply to the definition of the function. So, the `concatenate` function can be defined like this:

```
def concatenate text1, text2
  puts text1 + " " + text2
end
```

The second point is that the rule also applies to functions with no arguments – that is, we may remove the parenthesis from them, too. Let's take the following as an example:

```
return text.upcase()
```

This will now become the following:

```
return text.upcase
```

More importantly, the use of methods that use the question mark and destructive methods (`!`) now make perfect sense for readability.

Let's look at the following:

```
name.empty?()
```

This becomes as follows:

```
name.empty?
```

As another example, let's take the following:

```
name.upcase!()
```

This now becomes as follows:

```
name.upcase!
```

The last point we will look at now is related to how Ruby behaves with the return of values. While a method can explicitly return a value with the `return` keyword, Ruby doesn't need this keyword. Within functions and methods, Ruby automatically returns the last value that is referenced. Let's use the following example for this:

```
def to_upper text
  return text.upcase
end
```

That example would turn into this:

```
def to_upper text
  text.upcase
end
```

You will see a lot of Ruby code like this. It can be intimidating and confusing at first, but once you understand what Ruby is doing, it simply starts to make more sense.

As you have probably realized by now, Ruby's creator put a lot of emphasis on these tools to make it easier to write readable code. The community adopted this ideology and put it into practice. We not only see code using these conventions and rules to increment readability but we also see Ruby programmers adopt other conventions that, while they are not part of the Ruby rules per se, make perfect sense when used in context. I'm referring to variable and method naming. Because Ruby developers will try to make their code read like plain English, they will spend a lot of time thinking about how to name methods and variables to make the code more readable. For this reason, snake-case is more often used in Ruby, as it helps with readability. With that in mind, let's look at this example:

```
chocolate_allergy = true
puts "This person is allergic to chocolate"
  if chocolate_allergy
```

We can still improve its readability. And it wouldn't just be a syntactic change; it would also involve variable names and even defining a method, just to improve readability. So, a seasoned Ruby developer might write the final snippet for this example as follows:

```
def say text
  text
end
is_allergic = true
say "This person is allergic to chocolate" if is_allergic
```

As you can see, Ruby developers will go very far to make the code as readable as plain English. Of course, this is not always feasible and sometimes it's not practical as it at times requires putting a lot of effort into writing even something simple, but for the most part, as long as it's readable, by following these guidelines, other developers will thank you, not just the Ruby ones.

Summary

In this chapter, we covered the syntactic differences and similarities between PHP and Ruby, Ruby's tools for readability, and Ruby's syntactic flexibility. We also learned about the question mark (?) and the exclamation or bang symbol (!). Making it this far means that you are indeed trying to reuse your previous programming skills but with a new language: Ruby. This is a great start because you can skip one of the most difficult parts of learning a new language from scratch: the logical part. And while we've only seen the surface of Ruby, more importantly, we got a clear glimpse of how Ruby developers think when they're writing code. We learned that to a Ruby developer, readability comes first. We not only use syntax and language constructs to make this possible but we also use objects to increase the code's legibleness. The more it reads like a sentence, the better. We looked at some simple examples of Ruby, and while you could follow along, it was not the purpose of the exercise. It was more to pique your interest.

To move along on this learning path, we now need the proper tools to start writing and running Ruby code. In the next chapter, we will look at the different ways to install Ruby and set up our local environment so that we can start learning real examples of Ruby, and eventually follow along in the process.

2

Setting Up Our Local Environment

As a developer, you probably already know that one of the key skillsets that you need to start programming is to install the programming language itself onto your computer. We need a way to start testing code besides our head, as our brains are not the best language compilers. But what does installing the language really mean?

Coming from PHP, this could mean installing the binary interpreter of PHP on our computer so that we can run PHP, open a browser, and then away we go. Or it could mean downloading the PHP source code, compiling it, and generating our own binary with the compilation options we choose. In Ruby, we not only have very similar options to these, but also many more ways to install the Ruby interpreter on our local machine.

In this chapter, we will explore different ways of setting up our development environments. We will analyze the pros and cons of each to give you different options to choose from so that any errors will be consistent between developers, in order to avoid the wretched phrase all developers have heard and unfortunately used: *"It works on my machine."*

So, in this chapter, we will cover the following topics:

- Installing Ruby locally
- Using a virtual machine
- Using Docker
- Using rbenv

Technical requirements

To follow along with this chapter, we will need the following:

- Any IDE to view/edit code (e.g. SublimeText, Visual Studio Code, Notepad++ Vim, Emacs, etc.)

- For macOS users, you will also need to have the Xcode Command Line Tools installed

The code presented in this chapter is available at `https://github.com/PacktPublishing/From-PHP-to-Ruby-on-Rails`.

Installing Ruby locally

We are ready to set up our Ruby environment. Probably the most convenient way to install Ruby on our machines is with a package manager or an installer, depending on your operating system.

macOS users

For macOS users, the brew package manager is the way to go.

To install brew, using the Finder window, navigate to the **Applications** folder, then to the **Utilities** folder, and then scroll until you find **Terminal**:

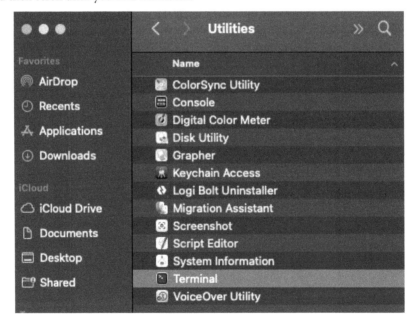

Figure 2.1: The Application Utilities

Double click on the **Terminal** icon and you should see a Terminal with a shell prompt waiting for commands:

```
[~ $ bash

The default interactive shell is now zsh.
To update your account to use zsh, please run `chsh -s /bin/zsh`.
For more details, please visit https://support.apple.com/kb/HT208050.
bash-3.2$
```

Figure 2.2: The Terminal

Then copy the command from the brew homepage (`https://brew.sh/`) that you can see here:

Figure 2.3: Homebrew installing instructions

Now paste the command into the Terminal to install brew.

Once brew is installed, installing Ruby (or its variations) is easy. If brew was already installed, you might just want to update it by running the `brew update` command. You may have to open up a new Terminal window, but once you've done that, you can install Ruby by simply running the following:

```
~ $ brew install ruby
```

This will result in the following output:

```
Running `brew update --auto-update`...
.
.
.
==> Summary
🍺  /opt/homebrew/Cellar/ruby/3.1.2_1: 15,996 files, 42.8MB
==> Running `brew cleanup ruby`...
Disable this behaviour by setting HOMEBREW_NO_INSTALL_CLEANUP.
Hide these hints with HOMEBREW_NO_ENV_HINTS (see `man brew`).
==> `brew cleanup` has not been run in the last 30 days, running
now...
Disable this behaviour by setting HOMEBREW_NO_INSTALL_CLEANUP.
```

```
.
.
.
Removing: /Users/bpineda/Library/Logs/Homebrew/gnutls... (64B)
Pruned 0 symbolic links and 6 directories from /opt/homebrew
==> Caveats
==> ruby
By default, binaries installed by gem will be placed into:
  /opt/homebrew/lib/ruby/gems/3.1.0/bin
You may want to add this to your PATh.
ruby is keg-only, which means it was not symlinked into /opt/homebrew,
because macOS already provides this software and installing another
version in
parallel can cause all kinds of trouble.

If you need to have ruby first in your PATH, run:
  ec'o 'export PA"H="/opt/homebrew/opt/ruby/bin:$P"'H"' >> /Users/
bpineda/.bash_profile

For compilers to find ruby you may need to set:
  export LDFLA"S="-L/opt/homebrew/opt/ruby/"ib"
  export CPPFLA"S="-I/opt/homebrew/opt/ruby/incl"de"
```

The code shown here has been redacted for brevity and may vary from version to version of macOS, but in essence, you should see the same (or very similar) output after brew has been installed. As long as there are no errors, you should be good to go. As a side note, I'd like to emphasize that brew is a package manager used by many developers working on macOS and some Linux environments, but it's not the only path to install Ruby.

As a last step we should open up a new Terminal window. This will load the $PATH variable again and make Ruby available for us to use. This a very pragmatic way of installing Ruby because we can start using the Ruby interpreter right away.

Now let's confirm that Ruby is in fact installed. In the Terminal, type the following:

```
ruby -v
```

This should return the Ruby version that was installed:

```
ruby 3.1.2p20 (2022-04-12 revision 4491bb740a) [arm64-darwin21]
```

We have successfully installed Ruby. Nowadays, most Macs already come with Ruby installed out of the box. However, it is an outdated version of Ruby, therefore it's still a good practice exercise to install it on our own.

Windows users

For Windows users, the simplest way to install Ruby is with an installer from `https://rubyinstaller.org/`:

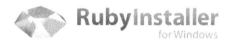

Downloads

RubyInstallers   Archives»

Not sure what version to download? Please read the right-hand column for recommendations.

WITH DEVKIT

=> Ruby+Devkit 3.1.2-1 (x64)   ≡
Ruby+Devkit 3.1.2-1 (x86)   ≡
Ruby+Devkit 3.0.4-1 (x64)   ≡
Ruby+Devkit 3.0.4-1 (x86)   ≡
Ruby+Devkit 2.7.6-1 (x64)   ≡
Ruby+Devkit 2.7.6-1 (x86)   ≡
Ruby+Devkit 2.6.10-1 (x64)   ≡
Ruby+Devkit 2.6.10-1 (x86)   ≡

Figure 2.4: Ruby Windows installer

I chose the latest version as it is best practice to install this one, or at least the latest stable version. Be sure to select the correct version (either 32-bit or 64-bit) depending on your machine architecture. Once it's downloaded, double-click on the installer and you will see this screen:

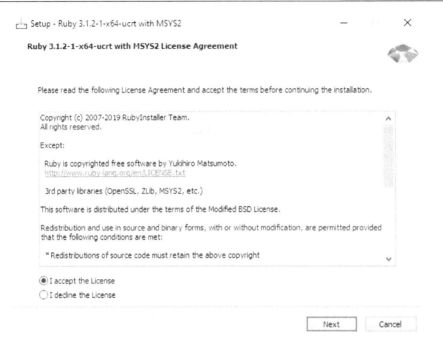

Figure 2.5: Windows Installer License Agreement

Accept the license and click **Next**.

Then choose the default options for the location and the addition of the binary to our PATH:

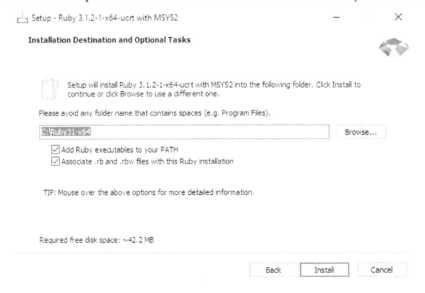

Figure 2.6: Windows Installer installation location

After that, select **Install**. Once this process is finished, we are prompted with a **Run 'ridk install'** option:

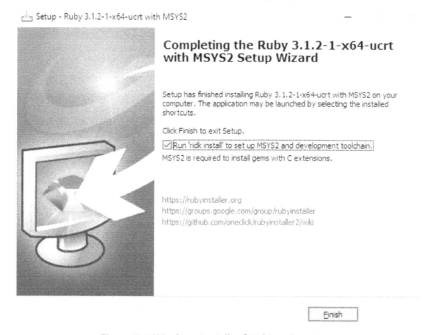

Figure 2.7: Windows Installer finishing the setup

While **Run 'ridk install'** is optional, I highly recommend it as it sets some environment variables and makes sh, make, and gcc available. These tools need to be compiled for some libraries (or gems) that we may use in the future. By setting this option, we will have another prompt pop up:

Figure 2.8: MSYS2 installation prompt

Press *Enter* for all options until the installation is done. These options install and update MSYS2, which provides a Unix-like environment for compatibility with software built on Windows systems.

Once done, make sure that Ruby was installed correctly. To do this, open Windows PowerShell. Then use the `ruby -v` command, and you should see the following:

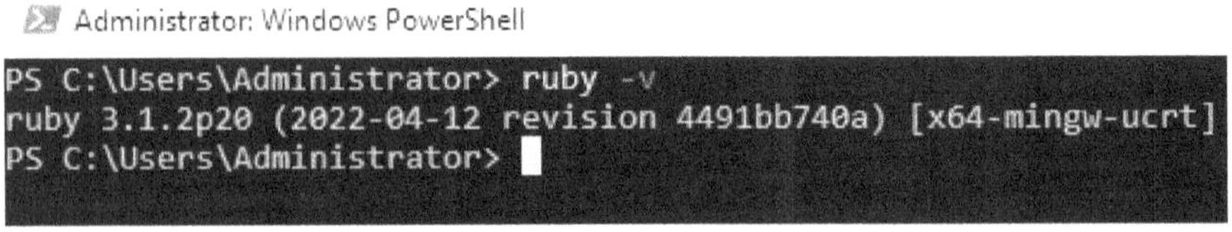

Figure 2.9: Windows Ruby version confirmation

With that, we have confirmed that Ruby is installed correctly on our Windows system.

Linux users

For Linux users, we have different distributions and while some of them share package managers, for the most part, each family uses its own package manager. As an example, the Red Hat family distros (Red Hat and CentOS) use `yum`, Ubuntu uses `apt`, and Debian uses `dpk` but also supports `apt`. We are going to focus on the most popular distribution used as a desktop operating system, which is Ubuntu.

In Ubuntu, navigate to the **Applications** window and open a **Terminal**. Once our Terminal is running, type `sudo apt install ruby`. Ubuntu will then confirm that you are in fact trying to install Ruby. When this confirmation comes up, just type *Y*, as you can see here:

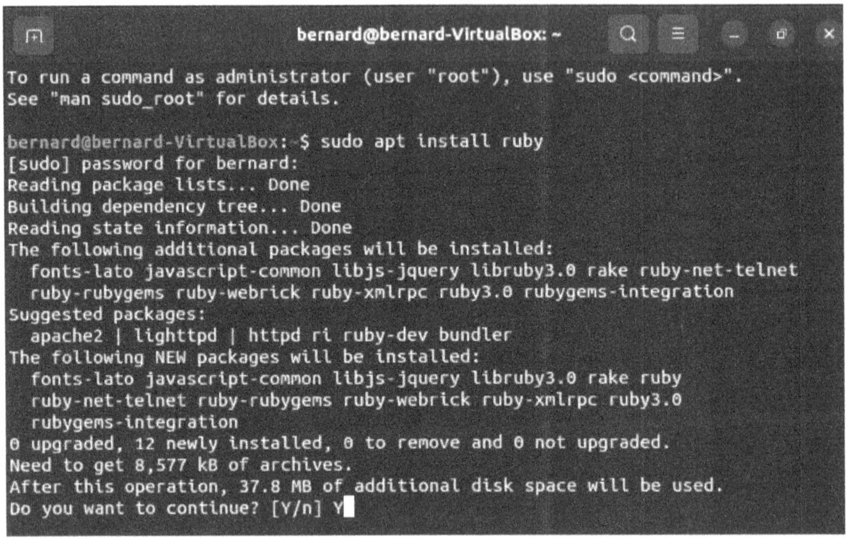

Figure 2.10: Ruby installation prompt

We use the `sudo` command because we require root privileges to install applications on our system. It might take a while to install depending on our internet speed and machine's specifications but once the process is finished, let's again verify the installation with `ruby -v`:

```
Setting up ruby3.0 (3.0.2-7ubuntu2.1) ...
Setting up ruby (1:3.0~exp1) ...
Setting up ruby-rubygems (3.3.5-2) ...
Processing triggers for man-db (2.10.2-1) ...
Processing triggers for fontconfig (2.13.1-4.2ubuntu5) ...
Processing triggers for libc-bin (2.35-0ubuntu3.1) ...
bernard@bernard-VirtualBox:~$ ruby -v
ruby 3.0.2p107 (2021-07-07 revision 0db68f0233) [x86_64-linux-gnu]
bernard@bernard-VirtualBox:~$
```

Figure 2.11: Ubuntu Ruby version confirmation

So, there we have it, you now know how to install Ruby on whichever operating system you use. Let's now take a look at using a virtual environment to work with Ruby.

Using a virtual machine

So far, we have seen how to install Ruby on our own local machine, that is, the machine we use daily for work. This is the best way to install Ruby when starting out, but once you start working on more complex applications and with other developers, you will want to have consistency in the behavior of everyone's local environments.

Why, you may ask? The simple answer is that we want to avoid the dreaded phrase that all developers have either heard or even used at some point in our careers: *"It works on my machine."* What is important to remember is that every local environment is different, from the processor to the OS version and Ruby version, and this can get in the way of more important work.

As an example that I personally experienced, we once wasted almost a week when we deployed a PHP application to a Linux server that was developed on Windows local machines. The problem was that one of the developers forgot that Windows (at the time) did not distinguish between uppercase and lowercase letters in folder names. While this might seem a silly example, we should try to avoid these issues as much as we can, as time can quickly be wasted while dealing with issues of this nature.

Virtualization can play an important role in the creation of equivalent environments between the developers in your team, and fortunately, we have several options that we can explore in the virtual realm to help us with this.

VMware

The first option is VMware (`https://vmware.com`). VMware lets you emulate a complete operating system within your machine. This setup, of course, takes longer than the others as you have to first install VMware, create a virtual machine, then install the operating system within this virtual machine, and then install Ruby. It would be certainly complex and time consuming, but once you have it up and running, you can share the environment with other members of your team. This would mean that everyone in the team would have the exact same environment.

VirtualBox

VirtualBox (`https://www.virtualbox.org`) is an Oracle product that behaves and has a similar workflow to VMware. Some people prefer VirtualBox and others prefer VMware. In my personal experience, VirtualBox is the better choice for beginners as it is open source, free to use, has a better UI, and works great for small to mid-sized projects.

Vagrant

Vagrant (`https://www.vagrantup.com/`) is a tool that helps us automate and manage our environments. Both VMware and VirtualBox have mechanisms in place to be able to share files and other resources with our host machine; however, they're not that easy to use, and sometimes it take up a lot of time to configure them. Vagrant comes in to solve that: it lets us specify shared folders between our local machine and the virtual one, allows us to replicate configurations through a configuration file, and also makes it much easier to connect to the virtual machine. The coolest part is that Vagrant can work seamlessly with both VMware and VirtualBox.

Laravel developers might be familiar with Vagrant as Homestead can be set up with VirtualBox. Even if you are not going to use this option as it may not be very practical, I would recommend at least trying it once to play around with Ruby on an operating system other than the one you have installed on your machine. This type of virtualization consumes a lot of resources, including memory, processor, and even disk space. It's a high price to pay for convenience, but worthwhile in the long run.

> **Note**
>
> As this goes beyond the scope of the book and is not necessary for initial Ruby developers; we will not be looking at how to carry out such installations. But it does make sense for a newbie Ruby developer to at least be familiar with these tools, only if by name. Should you be more curious about these implementations, particularly Vagrant and VirtualBox, you might want to head to the following site: `https://www.taniarascia.com/what-are-vagrant-and-virtualbox-and-how-do-i-use-them/`.

Lastly, there is a different type of virtualization provided by Docker, which is lighter than both VMware and VirtualBox, and this is what we will look at next.

Using Docker

Docker (`https://www.docker.com/`) is yet another virtualization technology that has become the go-to option for a lot of medium and large enterprises. While it's still a virtualized environment and comes with its own set of disadvantages, the advantages overshadow them. Let's take a look at a few advantages:

- Docker is not fully virtual – it creates a container that shares resources with the host in which it is running. Because of this, it runs significantly faster than a virtualized environment. I'm oversimplifying the Docker technology, but in essence it's an improved (in my opinion) virtualized environment.

- You can package your Docker environment into a Docker image (similar to a virtual machine), which can be deployed and used by others with ease.

- With the advent of cloud computing, Docker has become more and more popular. Amazon (AWS), Microsoft (Azure), and Google (GCP) all support Docker and little by little have made it much easier to implement.

- With Docker, you can replicate practically any error that occurred on another developer's machine, as well as in production environments (given the correct circumstances). Imagine a hypothetical developer world where you can take a production server and test things there, making sure that any error that was seen in the past is corrected before showing it to the public. Well, this is almost possible with Docker. Certainly, I'm simplifying the process, but essentially, the Docker image you use locally has the potential to be the same image used in production.

The main disadvantage with Docker is that it's more complicated to understand how to use images and containers and build microservices. If you've never heard of microservices, the concept might take you aback as they are different than traditional applications and deployments. Microservices are an architectural style used to build applications by separating the application into a collection of services. Docker Compose might make it easier to implement microservices locally, but it's still a complex topic.

> **Note**
>
> Should you be more interested in the topic of microservices, you should take look at `https://microservices.io/`.

I honestly think it's worth exploring Docker more than other virtualization options simply because it's gained so much popularity among the developer and infrastructure communities.

While we won't take a deep dive into Docker, we can take some baby steps to learn how to use it on our local environment. The first step is to install Docker through an installer or package manager. Depending on your OS and distribution, use one of the following:

- For Mac: `https://docs.docker.com/desktop/install/mac-install/`

- For Windows: `https://docs.docker.com/desktop/install/windows-install/`

- For Linux: `https://docs.docker.com/desktop/install/linux-install/`

After that, we can run the following command to verify that Docker has been installed:

```
docker -v
```

This should return the current Docker version found on your machine:

```
Docker version 20.10.17, build 100c701
```

Once Docker is available, we can download a Ruby image and run a Ruby command with this one liner:

```
docker run --entrypoint ruby ruby:latest -v
```

Here, we are telling the Docker agent to get the latest Ruby Docker image and then run `ruby -v`. The command should output something similar to this:

```
Unable to find image 'ruby:latest' locally
latest: Pulling from library/ruby
cd84405c8b9e: Pull complete
a1d98e120b80: Pull complete
7cb6be5911b4: Pull complete
db608c3c3ce3: Pull complete
ef10f752bfb9: Pull complete
65032c8238ec: Pull complete
a6196a66f1a5: Pull complete
8f0e459675ce: Pull complete
Digest:
sha256:74f02cae856057841964d471f0a54a5957dec7079cfe18076c132ce5
c6b6ea37
Status: Downloaded newer image for ruby:latest
ruby 3.1.2p20 (2022-04-12 revision 4491bb740a) [aarch64-linux]
```

The first time you run this command, it might take a while because it will have to download the Ruby Docker image. Once the Docker image is downloaded, it starts a container with said image and runs the command. Once the command has been run, the container is halted.

And with that, we have successfully run a Ruby command with Docker. While actually using Docker for development in a more practical way is more complicated, this is a great starting point.

Now that we've seen a couple of options to set up our local environment, we'll move to the next essential tool for Ruby development, that is, rbenv.

Using rbenv

While it is highly recommended to use some sort of homogeneous environment for all members of the team (such as the virtual ones previously mentioned), a simpler and quicker way to create equivalent environments is to use some sort of Ruby version management tool. These types of tools allow us to install different versions of Ruby and for the most part will behave similarly, even if they are installed on different operating systems. We have a couple of options, but for simplicity, we will use rbenv: `https://github.com/rbenv/rbenv`.

rbenv allows us to install multiple versions of Ruby and manage these versions. By *managing them*, I mean we can define what version of Ruby the whole system uses (global), or we can define a specific version to be used on each project (local). For macOS and Linux users, you should follow the instructions on the previously mentioned GitHub repository, which also serves as the official website. If you run into any issues while trying to install the tool, you could also follow these two tutorials for installing rbenv:

- `https://www.digitalocean.com/community/tutorials/how-to-install-ruby-on-rails-with-rbenv-on-macos`

- `https://collectionbuilder.github.io/cb-docs/docs/software/ruby_mac/`

Lastly, for Windows users, we have rbenv-for-windows: `https://github.com/ccmywish/rbenv-for-windows`.

Beware that the version for Windows might be a little limited and you may encounter issues with certain versions of Ruby.

Once we've installed rbenv, we should list the Ruby versions we have installed on the machine. Let's open a shell and run the following command:

```
rbenv versions
```

This should show the following output:

```
* system
```

The preceding output means that we only have one version of Ruby installed. Let's add Ruby 2.6.10 to use throughout the examples of this book. We'll do so by typing the following command on the shell:

```
rbenv install 2.6.10
```

This should throw the following output:

```
To follow progress, use 'tail -f /var/folders/47/x76117cd0419z61zb_
kt7yzc0000gn/T/ruby-build.20231019202743.61499.log' or pass -verbose
...
Downloading ruby-2.6.10.tar.bz2...
-> https://cache.ruby-lang.org/pub/ruby/2.6/ruby-2.6.10.tar.bz2
Installing ruby-2.6.10...
...
NOTE: to activate this Ruby version as the new default, run: rbenv
global 2.6.10
```

Now that we have Ruby 2.6.10 available for use, we can start using said version with the following command:

```
rbenv local 2.6.10
```

Once the preceding command has been run, make sure to test it with the following command:

```
ruby --version
```

This should show the current version of Ruby to be 2.6.10:

```
ruby 2.6.10p210 (2022-04-12 revision 67958) [arm64-darwin22]
```

The output may vary from system to system, but the version should be the same. I won't dwell too much on how rbenv works, but I will say that by running this command on a folder, any work you do while in said folder (or subfolders within this folder) will have Ruby 2.6.10 for use. If we move to a different folder, the Ruby version available will be different. It's an important best practice to set the Ruby version for each project and not just rely on the one installed on the computer. Switching Ruby versions is now as easy as installing the required version and applying said version with the aforementioned command. For the exercises in this book, I highly recommend relying on rbenv.

As an alternative to rbenv, we have rvm: https://rvm.io/.

However, I highly recommend choosing rbenv over rvm as most developers use rbenv. You can give rvm a try, if you're up to the challenge.

Summary

So far, we've learned how to install Ruby on macOS, Windows, and Linux systems. While some operating systems may already come with Ruby installed, it is almost always outdated. We should always install the latest version of Ruby, as installing Ruby is part of our own development process as Ruby developers.

We also learned about virtualization with VMware, VirtualBox, and Docker. I want to point out that the theory regarding virtualization technologies might be a little overwhelming for a beginner developer – I personally did not work with any of these virtual technologies when I started with Ruby, mainly because it was not a practical option, but also because they had not become so popular at that time – but I can now confidently say that I wish I had had those resources when I started, as it would have saved me some major headaches. Having said that, I can guarantee you that they will come in handy (at least Docker), but to start programming in Ruby they are not compulsory. Lastly, we learned about rbenv, its basic commands, and why it has become the go-to Ruby version manager in the Ruby community.

Moving on to our next chapter, we are now ready to start writing some Ruby ourselves. We will also take a look at the Ruby syntax compared to PHP and analyze how we can take advantage of what we already know from PHP and port it to Ruby. Lastly, we will learn about the Ruby language enhancements that PHP does not have but which make perfect sense in the Ruby world.

3

Comparing Basic Ruby Syntax to PHP

Running scripts in PHP and Ruby is similar, though each language has its peculiarities. Similarly, both Ruby's and PHP's syntax can be strangely similar at times, as we saw in *Chapter 1*. However, if we are serious about becoming Ruby programmers, we will need to learn both the differences and the enhancements that Ruby brings to the table.

Let's embark on this journey and start creating, executing, and debugging our own Ruby scripts with the resources that we already have from knowing PHP, and see Ruby's language improvements over other languages. We'll not only think in Ruby but program in "the Ruby way" too.

So, in this chapter, we will cover the following topics:

- Running Ruby code from the command line
- Exploring types of variables
- Using conditional statements
- Repeating code with loops
- Using Ruby language enhancements

Technical requirements

To follow along with this chapter, we will need the following:

- Any IDE to view/edit code (for example, SublimeText, Visual Studio Code, Notepad++ Vim, Emacs, and so on)
- For macOS users, you will also need to have Xcode Command Line Tools installed
- Ruby version 2.6 or later will need to be installed and ready to use

The code presented in this chapter is available at `https://github.com/PacktPublishing/From-PHP-to-Ruby-on-Rails/`.

Running Ruby code from the command line

One of the first things we need to learn about when picking up Ruby is how to run our code and view the output directly on our screen. There are different ways to achieve this, but we will be doing so in the simplest of ways. While there are various ways to load code from the command line, we'll start with one single file.

Running a simple code file

As I mentioned in the introduction, running scripts in Ruby is simple and easy. Similar to running scripts in PHP, we can create a file, add Ruby code to it, and execute it with Ruby. Running or executing code simply means that we will have Ruby read (also referred to as parse) through our source code, and then translate it into a language that the computer can understand and process.

Let's start with a simple example by creating a folder called `ruby_syntax` on our desktop. In that folder, create our source code file, which is called `running_ruby.rb`, with your IDE of choice.

Now, let's add some code to our file:

```
# running_ruby.rb
print('I am running a Ruby script');
```

Now, let's open a shell and go to the same folder we just created:

```
cd path-to-our-desktop/ruby_syntax
```

Once we are in this folder in our shell, we can run the script we just created with Ruby:

```
ruby running_ruby.rb
```

This should output the following:

```
I am running a Ruby script
```

As I mentioned in *Chapter 1*, this syntax is strangely familiar to the PHP one. If we compared the two, we would have the following PHP equivalent:

```
<?php # running_php.php
print('I am running a PHP script');
```

We would then run the example in the same way as the Ruby one, but with the PHP executable instead, like so:

```
php running_php.php
```

The outcome would be the same as the Ruby one but with the string for PHP.

Back to the Ruby example, and just like we did to the examples in *Chapter 1*, let's modify our Ruby code so that it's slightly more readable:

```
# running_ruby.rb
print 'I am running a Ruby script without parenthesis'
```

Even though the syntax is slightly similar, the outcome is the same, with the advantage that it reads more naturally. While print is available in Ruby for outputting text for the user, you may also use puts or simply p. You'll see this very often in Ruby.

Loading a source code file with the load method

At this point, you know how to execute Ruby code in a single file. However, as our source code grows, it will become impractical to have a single source code file. That is why Ruby allows us to load source code from other source files.

Let's see how to do this. First, we must create a file to be loaded – in this example, the file is called my_library.rb and contains some simple content:

```
# my_library.rb
print 'I am a library.'
```

While we now have runnable Ruby code, we are not going to run my_library.rb directly, but rather let another script load its code. This is where the load method comes in. The load method takes a filename and its code and includes it in our execution. So, let's create another file called load_library.rb with this content:

```
# load_library.rb
load 'my_library.rb'
```

Now, run the code with the following command:

```
ruby load_library.rb
```

The output of the script should be as follows:

```
I am a library.
```

The `load_library.rb` file injects (or as its name implies, *loads*) the code from the `my_library.rb` file and executes it. This way, we can easily separate large chunks of code into smaller, more readable ones.

Now, what happens if we call the `load` method more than once in Ruby? Well, let's try it out:

```
# load_library.rb
load 'my_library.rb'
load 'my_library.rb'
```

After running the command again, the output is as follows:

```
I am a library. I am a library.
```

From this behavior, we can infer that every time we load a file, its code will be executed, which is very useful when our files change multiple times during their execution – in these cases, the code is said to be dynamically changing.

As an example of dynamically changing code, let's say we needed a script to include new parts of the code, but could not be stopped for doing so. In a case such as this, we would need the code to be constantly refreshed, and this is where the `load` method comes in. The `load` method refreshes the code every single time it comes across the file that's changing – that is, it renews our code every time the Ruby engine detects a change. Otherwise, we would have to stop the execution every time we needed a new change in our code.

Ruby's `load` method is similar to PHP's `include` and `require` functions. However, Ruby's `require` method is slightly different than the one in PHP, as we'll see next.

Loading a source code file with the require method

In contrast to the `load` method, sometimes, we just need the code to be executed only once, and for that, we can use the `require` method.

Let's see it in action by creating another file called `require_library.rb` with the following content:

```
# require_library.rb
require './my_library.rb'
```

Now, let's run it in the same way that we ran the `load_library.rb` script:

```
ruby require_library.rb
```

Initially, the output will be the same as when we ran the `load_library.rb` script:

```
I am a library.
```

However, notice that in this example, we included the dot slash prefix (./) before the filename. The `require` function needs either the absolute path or the relative path of the file – because the `my_library.rb` example is within the same folder, we use the relative path to the current folder, which would be ./. In simple terms, the source code for `require_library.rb` would read as "inject the code that is in the `my_library.rb` file, which is in the same folder."

Now, let's try calling the `require` method more than once:

```
# require_library.rb
require './my_library.rb'
require './my_library.rb'
```

Let's run it again with the following code:

```
ruby require_library.rb
```

To an experienced PHP developer, it should not be a surprise that the output is as follows:

```
I am a library.
```

Ruby's `require` method works pretty much the same way as `include_once` and `require_once` from PHP. The Ruby interpreter only loads the code once, and whenever you try to load it again, the engine notices that you already loaded that code, so it doesn't load it again, saving memory and resources.

One last thing we may wish to consider while using the `require` method is that it is not compulsory to include the file extension, so this will also work:

```
# require_library.rb
require './my_library'
```

By not using the file extension, our code looks slightly cleaner. Now, how is the `require` method useful, you may ask? Well, whenever you're writing libraries that will be used in several parts of your code, you don't have to worry about loading your library multiple times as the `require` method will only load it once, thus saving memory resources. We'll keep it simple for now, but if you are interested in more options for importing code, there is also the `require_relative` method: https://apidock.com/ruby/Kernel/require_relative.

Ruby classes and modules

In Ruby, modules are a way to group code so that it can be reused. Specifically, modules are collections of methods and constants that can be injected into classes. By themselves, modules aren't useful as you can't use them in an isolated manner. We use modules to add functionality to a class.

A class, as you probably know, is a blueprint of an abstraction from the real world taken to the programming world. A class can have different methods to represent actions and attributes to represent values. A class can be enhanced by including additional methods and constants from a module. So, in simple terms, a class can attach methods and constants from a module – and that's what the include method does.

Let's look at this in a simplified example. Create a file called include_module.rb with the following code:

```
# include_module.rb
class MyClass end
```

Here, we're creating a simple empty class called MyClass with no methods. Now, let's create an instance of this class:

```
my_class_instance = MyClass.new
```

We can't do much with this class as it is empty, so let's add a Utilities module to it:

```
module Utilities end
```

And just like the previous class (MyClass), this is just an empty module. Let's add a method called debug to our module so that both our class and module end up looking like this:

```
# include_module.rb
class MyClass end
module Utilities
  def debug
    puts 'We are debugging'
  end
end
my_class_instance = MyClass.new
```

With this code, we've declared a method named debug that prints the text "We are debugging." Can we add this method to MyClass? Well, this is where the include method comes in.

The include method

At this point, we should incorporate this newly built debug method with the include method because, as it stands now, the debug method is not currently being used. It's merely defined. With the include method, we can now "attach" the debug method to our class by adding this to the end of the file:

```
MyClass.include(Utilities)
```

This simply means that the `debug` method is now available to `my_class_instance`. Let's call our newly included `debug` method from our class instance. Your final code should look like this:

```
# include_module.rb
class MyClass end
module Utilities
  def debug
    puts 'We are debugging'
  end
end
my_class_instance = MyClass.new
MyClass.include(Utilities)
my_class_instance.debug
```

Now, for the moment of truth – let's run it:

```
ruby require_library.rb
```

This will output the following:

```
We are debugging
```

This means that we have successfully attached the debug method to our empty class. This comes in handy whenever we need modules that are reused throughout our code.

The equivalent to Ruby's `include` method in PHP is a resource called `traits`. If you're interested in this topic, check out `https://www.php.net/manual/en/language.oop5.traits.php`. This might be a little complicated to grasp at first since we haven't looked at object-oriented programming in Ruby so far, but don't worry if you don't fully understand it at this point – we will get there.

Interactive Ruby Shell (IRB)

Sometimes, you may want to quickly test a very small piece of code and it may seem like a hassle to create a file, add the code, and then run it. Maybe we just want to test the syntax of a single line of code. Well, we don't have to create a file to just test a line of code. Just like in other languages, such as Python or even PHP, we have a tool just for that in Ruby: it's the **Interactive Ruby Shell**, better known as **IRB**. Let's take a look at it.

Within a shell, run the following command:

```
irb
```

This will make your shell look like this:

```
irb(main):001:0>
```

This shell works as a real-time Ruby interpreter – that is, after the > symbol, we can start typing Ruby commands that will be interpreted and executed right away. As a simple example, let's add 1 and 1:

```
irb(main):001:0> 1+1
```

This will return the following result:

```
irb(main):001:0> 1+1
=> 2
```

This comes in quite handy when you quickly want to test syntax and operations, or even view the content of a class. It works in the same way as the Ruby binary we've been using in previous examples.

So, as a final example, let's load the include_module file we created, but now with this interactive shell:

```
irb(main):001:0> require './include_module'
We are debugging
=> true
```

Now that we've included the code in our shell with the require method, we can use this loaded code in our irb session. Since we have the MyClass definition available, we can use it as a blueprint to create an instance of MyClass:

```
irb(main):001:0> another_instance = MyClass.new
```

This returns a unique identifier that Ruby uses internally to know where the instance resides in the computer's memory:

```
=> #<MyClass:0x000000014a17ed50>
```

Note that we can call the debug method on our newly created instance too:

```
irb(main):001:0> another_instance.debug
```

And just like before, we get the same output:

```
We are debugging
=> nil
```

To exit this interactive shell, simply type exit to make your shell go back to normal. In case you were wondering, there is a similar shell in PHP called interactive shell. Be sure to check out this page if you're interested in this topic: https://www.php.net/manual/en/features.commandline.interactive.php.

At this point, we can proudly say that we now know how to run Ruby code in a couple of different ways. We also know how to use a single source code file, or load code from a separate source code file. Either way, whether you're running your code with the Ruby binary or with the interactive shell, you're going to need a way to store and use values, which brings us to our next topic: variables.

Exploring types of variables

Variables in Ruby have the same utility as in other programming languages: they are mutable containers for values. Simply put, variables are used to save values for later usage. These values may change over time, or even change the type of data they contain.

Just like with PHP, Ruby is dynamically typed (or duck typing), which means that the interpreter infers what type of data we are handling at runtime. We don't need to tell Ruby or PHP that a variable is either a string, a number, or a Boolean. One difference with PHP, however, is that in later versions of PHP, you *can* specify what type of data to use, especially in object-oriented PHP. However, even with this "enhancement," the majority of the language remains duck-typed.

How does this affect us as developers? Well, let's take a look at a simple example. First, open an IRS. Type the following command:

```
irb
```

As we saw previously, once we type this command, the shell will look like this:

```
irb(main):001:0>
```

Now, type the following declarations:

```
name = "Oscar"
age = 35
is_married = true
books_read_this_week = 2.5
```

Note that though the information in the previous code block is what you should type, it will look like this in the prompt:

```
irb(main):001:0> name = "Oscar"
=> "Oscar"
irb(main):002:0> age = 35
=> 35
irb(main):003:0> is_married = true
=> true
irb(main):004:0>books_read_this_week = 2.5
=> 2.5
```

One of the core features of the Ruby language is that with every line of code, Ruby will attempt to return a value. If you declare a variable, Ruby will return the assigned value. So, when we added the name variable, Ruby returned the value of the variable – that is, "Oscar". This comes in handy when we use this behavior to obtain the type of data a variable is holding. Ruby "knows" what type of data this name variable contains.

To do this, we can make use of the internal `class` method. Just type `name.class`; `irb` should return something similar to this:

```
irb(main):005:0> name.class
=> String
```

The Ruby interpreter determined that the `name` variable is a string, or in simple terms, text. The same can be done to the other variables we just declared, such as the `age` variable:

```
irb(main):006:0> age.class
=> Integer
```

And in that same manner, the `is_married` variable is a Boolean variable. We can confirm this by getting the class of that variable:

```
irb(main):006:0> is_married.class
=> TrueClass
```

This means that the `is_married` variable has a Boolean value of `true`. We can do the same with the `books_read_this_week` variable:

```
irb(main):006:0> books_read_this_week.class
=> Float
```

We did not explicitly tell Ruby what type of variables we were going to use, yet Ruby "knew" this automagically. This means that we don't have to worry about telling Ruby the type of data we are going to use. This is pragmatic for the most part, but I must admit I've been in scenarios where it would have helped to have known the type of data before runtime.

So far, in our previous examples, we've looked at four different types of variables in Ruby: strings, integers, Booleans (true or false), and float values. However, there are three more types of variables that we should look at in depth: arrays, hashes, and symbols. We'll go through each of them now.

Arrays

Arrays are a way of grouping common variables. Coming from a PHP background, arrays can be very simple to understand both conceptually and syntactically. Conceptually, we put together similar or related values. An example could be grouping a person's phone numbers in a single variable. Another example could be storing a physical address by saving the street, number, city, zip code, and more all in the same variable. As we will see next, the Ruby syntax is very similar to the PHP one.

Arrays let us take related values and save them in a single variable. As an example, let's say we wanted to save my siblings' ages. We could create an array of integers that represented my siblings' ages. Let's do just that in PHP and Ruby and compare both syntaxes. This would be the PHP syntax:

```
$siblings_ages = [ 42, 31, 25 ];
```

And this would be the Ruby syntax:

```
siblings_ages = [ 42, 31, 25 ]
```

Except for $ and ; ,, both pieces of code are the same; this goes to show that understanding the concepts of Ruby arrays should not be difficult if you're from a PHP background. While there are other ways to declare arrays, we'll keep the syntax simple for now.

Now that we understand how to declare arrays, let's look at some practical uses for them.

Arrays can have other types of values in Ruby (not just numbers). Let's say I wanted to list the instruments someone knows how to play. We could make a list of strings and name it `instruments_played`:

```
instruments_played = ["guitar", "drums", "bass", "ukulele"]
```

As you can see, we have grouped related values (in this case instruments) in a single variable. We've created a list ready to be used within our code. This type of array, as it was declared, has an internal counter to reference each value. This internal counter starts with 0, so the first value (`guitar`) would be contained in `instruments_played[0]`, the second value (`drums`) would be contained in `instruments_played[1]`, and so on.

Should we want to print out all of the instruments on the screen, we could print each instrument one by one:

```
puts instruments_played[0]
puts instruments_played[1]
puts instruments_played[2]
puts instruments_played[3]
```

However, this is tedious and impractical, and as you may have guessed, we have a better programming way of doing this. Instead of counting one by one, we can iterate through all values of the array using the `do` statement:

```
for i in 0...4 do
puts instruments_played[i]
end
```

The three-dot notation (...) might be new and even weird to someone coming from PHP, but if you just read through the code, it almost makes sense. This notation is called range and you'll see it used often in Ruby. The notation creates a counter that goes from 0 to a value less than 4 (3, in this case), then increments the counter by 1. This counter is then assigned to the `i` variable. The example would read something like, "For the `i` variable, create a cycle that starts with 0, ends in 3, increases by 1, and prints each value of the array one by one." The output would look something like this:

```
guitar
drums
```

```
bass
ukulele
=> 0...4
```

Did you notice that the ... notation excludes the number 4, equivalent to [0,4] in mathematical notation? Well, what if we wanted the range to be inclusive – for example, [0,3] – which would include the last number? Ruby also has a two-dot notation (..) that *does* include the last number in its range. So, we could rewrite the example as follows:

```
for i in 0..3 do
puts instruments_played[i]
end
```

The output would be the same as the previous example:

```
guitar
drums
bass
ukulele
=> 0..3
```

You may use the three-dot or the two-dot notation as you see fit. If you are more interested in the topic of ranges, I suggest that you look at the documentation regarding this topic: https://ruby-doc.org/core-2.5.1/Range.html.

Now, let's get back to arrays. Just like PHP, Ruby has some internal methods to work with arrays. As an example of this parallel design, PHP has a function to tell us the size of an array. The function is called count() and has a Ruby equivalent called size(). Just remember that everything in Ruby is an object, so you would not use size(instruments_played) as you would in PHP. Instead, to print the number of elements of our array, we would call the size() method as a method of the instruments_played array:

```
puts instruments_played.size
```

Since the array has four elements, we would get an output of 4. Additionally, there is another method that does the same thing called length.

Two more internal methods that I find extremely useful are first and last. These methods (as we can infer from their names) let us fetch the first and last elements of the array, respectively. Let's try the first method with some variable interpolation:

```
puts "I learned how to play the #{instruments_played.first} first"
```

This would output the following:

```
I learned how to play the guitar first
```

The `last` method works in the same way:

```
puts "I learned how to play the #{instruments_played.last} last"
```

This would output as expected:

```
I learned how to play the ukulele last
```

As you can see, we've combined a string and a variable's content to create a new string. This combination is referred to as variable interpolation.

Variable interpolation

Variable interpolation (a term you will hear a lot in programming) involves substituting a variable with its value. It's extremely useful when printing messages and/or showing data to users. When used correctly, variable interpolation lets us embed a variable value inside a string. Let's take the code from our previous example:

```
instruments_played = ["guitar", "drums", "bass", "ukulele"]
puts "I learned how to play the #{instruments_played.first} first"
```

There are a couple of layers to the string interpolation feature, so let's analyze it in parts.

First, on the second line of the code, we can see that, inside the string, we have added a special block, which starts with the # symbol followed by a set of curly brackets (#{ }). When used inside a string, this block determines that we are going to use interpolation.

Secondly, everything inside the curly brackets will be interpreted and returned. In this example, the code inside the curly brackets is `instruments_played.last`, which holds the last element of the array. This last element of the array will be returned as part of the string, thus finalizing the interpolation. This only works when the string is defined with double quotes ("").

Combining array types

So far, we've seen arrays that hold the same type of data – we had an array exclusively made of strings and another array exclusively made of integers. But one last feature worth noting regarding Ruby arrays is that they can also combine different variable types within the same array. As a random example, let's add unrelated values to an array:

```
random_values = [25, "drums", false, 3.8]
```

In this array, we are combining different types of data (integers, strings, Booleans, and floating points) into a single array. Not all languages support this behavior within arrays, but both Ruby and PHP do.

As we mentioned when we started looking at variable types, Ruby is dynamically typed. One of the features of a dynamically typed language is that arrays can combine the type of data they hold. In contrast, in a strongly typed language such as Java, arrays are forced to have the same type of data on each element – that is, you can only have an array of integers or only an array of strings. That is not to say that Ruby is better than Java or that, in general, strongly typed languages are better than dynamically typed languages. They just have different designs.

If you're interested in learning more regarding the subject of arrays, please take a look at the official Ruby documentation: `https://ruby-doc.org/core-2.7.0/Array.html`.

Hashes

Now, let's take a look at another type of variable that PHP developers will also understand very easily: hashes. A hash is an array but the main difference is that it has textual indexes instead of numbered indexes. Hashes are very similar to arrays in their behavior, but with the difference that we use strings to reference certain values. In PHP, these are known as associative arrays.

Let's see an example in action. Here, we have a hash with the index in English and the value in Spanish:

```
numbers = { "one" => "uno", "two" => "dos", "three" => "tres" }
```

Similar to what we could do with an array, to get the value of a single index, we could type the following:

```
puts numbers["one"]
```

We would get the following output:

```
uno
```

As you can see, the index is a string and is more readable to a human. It's this readability where a hash can come in handy. Let's rewrite the first example we used at the start of the *Exploring types of variables* section so that it uses a hash:

```
person = { "name" => "Oscar", "age" => 35, "is_married" => true,
"books_read_this_week" => 2.5 }
```

Instead of having separate variables for `name`, `age`, `is_married`, and `books_read_this_week`, we have a hash that groups all of these values into a single variable called `person`. Now, we can reference each index, as follows:

```
person["name"]
person["age"]
person["is_married"]
person["books_read_this_week"]
```

Additionally, we could print a very readable message with the following:

```
puts "#{person["name"]} is #{person["age"]} years old"
```

Even for a developer who is just starting Ruby, this is not just readable but understandable regarding the intent of the code. As expected, it would output the following:

```
Oscar is 35 years old
```

Hashes are super useful when working with mapped data that needs to be read by a human. It's also useful when you're working with data that is changing.

This brings us to the last variable type that we're going to see, which I must say is more complicated than I wish it were. The types of variables we've seen so far are mutable, which means that they can be changed. However, sometimes, we don't need certain values to change – we need more of a location where this value is stored. Symbols do just this.

Symbols

Symbols are highly optimized identifiers that map immutable strings to fixed internal values. They are also immutable strings themselves – that is, they do not change their value.

The concept is a bit complex, but I believe it will be more understandable with an example. Let's take a simple string and view what its value is pointing to. So, run this code:

```
"name".object_id
```

When you create a string, Ruby will take the string object and internally save it somewhere in memory. The `object_id` method saves this internal unique identifier. Notice what happens when you call the same line a couple of times:

```
irb(main):126:0> "name".object_id
=> 2391267760
irb(main):127:0> "name".object_id
=> 2391332180
irb(main):128:0> "name".object_id
=> 2391359800
```

The first string is pointing to a different address than the second and third strings. So, every time we type the `name` string, Ruby creates and stores a brand new string. Even though they have the same value, they are still different. As an analogy, it would be like having a file with the same name but in different folders. Even if the files had the same contents, they are still different files.

This is not the same with symbols. Symbols refer to the same memory location. Let's try the same example with symbols:

```
:name.object_id
```

This should also return a unique identifier number. However, what happens when we call this same code multiple times?

```
Irb(main):129:0> :name.object_id
=> 88028
irb(main):130:0> :name.object_id
=> 88028
irb(main):131:0> :name.object_id
=> 88028
```

Instead of returning different random numbers, this time, we get the same (though still random) number. This is because every time we call :name, the Ruby interpreter is looking at the same location in memory. Using the same analogy, it would be like creating a unique file, and then whenever we needed the file again, we would create links that would point to that original file. So, even if the links were in different folders, they would point to the same file.

We won't dive into this subject further for now as it's enough to just understand the basics of it, but we will see more examples in future chapters, particularly the Ruby on Rails ones. At the moment, just remember this good rule of thumb: use a symbol when the identity of an object is important. Should the content be more important, use a string.

If you would like to know more about symbols now, the following website is a great resource: `https://medium.com/@lcriswell/ruby-symbols-vs-strings-248842529fd9`.

So far, we've learned all about variables. But what good is a variable if we can't make decisions regarding these variables? That's our next topic.

Using conditional statements

Now that we know what types of variables we can use in Ruby, let's give these variables some more practical use.

The if statement

By now, we should all be familiar with the `if` statement and its structure: if a sentence is true, the code should do or return something.

Let's take the person hash that we used in the previous section as our base:

```
person = { "name" => "Oscar", "age" => 35, "is_married" => true,
"books_read_this_week" => 2.5 }
```

Using that, we can create a basic `if` statement:

```
if person["is_married"] == true
  puts "Person is married"
end
```

This is pretty much self-explanatory. This would read: "If the value in `person["married"]` is equal to true, then print `Person is married`." The end keyword limits when the `if` statement is done – that is, anything after the `end` keyword is not part of the block. You'll see the end key keyword a lot in Ruby – just keep in mind that it is used to delimit certain blocks of code.

While the previous code is useful, there is a better way to write this – the "Ruby way." First, we remove `== true` and if we are only going to execute a single action, we can write it in one line:

```
puts "Person is married" if person["is_married"]
```

This reads much like a sentence and you'll see a lot of Rubyists using this useful one-liner.

The if-else statement

If you need a different action in case the value is not true, then you should use the `if-else` structure:

```
if person["age"] < 31
  puts "This person is under 30"
else
  puts "This person is over 30"
end
```

This would output the following:

```
This person is over 30
```

Just remember, the `if` statement evaluates the condition. If the condition is true, Ruby executes the code that is on the next line. However, if the condition is false, Ruby skips the first block, goes to the `else` statement, and executes the code that is right after the `else` keyword.

The ternary operator

As a last example of the `if` statement, we also have the ternary operator, which we also have in other coding languages; though it's not as readable, it's still useful. Let's see an example:

```
over_or_under = person["age"] > 31 ? "over" : "under"
puts "This person is #{over_or_under} 30"
```

With the ternary operator, the condition between the = sign and ? will be evaluated. If the condition is deemed as true, then the value to the left of the : symbol is returned. If the condition is deemed as false, then the value to the right of the : symbol is returned. In this case, the value stored in person["age"] is 35. Since 35 is over 30, the over string will be stored in the over_or_under variable. The second line of code will simply interpolate this value and should return this:

```
This person is over 30
```

While this is not as readable as the previous if statements, the code is still valid and available in most programming languages. The ternary operator is the same in PHP and is useful when you need to store a value that depends on a condition.

The if statement is probably one of the most used resources in programming, so it's a good idea to understand the syntax, the use, and the different use cases that it solves. Now, let's look at another resource that uses true/false values to run code.

Repeating code with loops

We have come to our next topic, which is loops. Ruby, just like other languages, has different ways of making the same code execute repeatedly. When we discussed arrays, specifically the array that contained instruments' names, we saw an example of the for loop, which was used to print each instrument contained in the array. But let's look at another type of loop, one that is more commonly used: the while loop.

The while loop lets us repeat a code execution that is determined by a true/false condition. Let's say we wanted to print a number from one to three. We could create a print statement and simply repeat it three times while incrementing the value. However, let's try a different way that will be more concise. Start by creating a counter variable:

```
counter = 1
```

Now, we can start the while loop cycle:

```
while counter <= 3
  puts counter
  counter++
end
```

This may seem like valid code, but we will get an error from the Ruby interpreter:

```
Traceback (most recent call last):
        3: from /usr/bin/irb:23:in `<main>'
        2: from /usr/bin/irb:23:in `load'
```

```
        1: from /Library/Ruby/Gems/2.6.0/gems/irb-1.0.0/exe/irb:11:in
`<top (required)>'
SyntaxError ((irb):205: syntax error, unexpected end)
```

This is because of a common erroneous assumption that most Ruby newbies make. If you use PHP or JavaScript, you will be used to the ++ operator, which is equivalent to adding 1 to a variable. It's the same as writing the following:

```
counter = counter + 1
```

However, the ++ operator does not exist in Ruby (so this also goes for the −− operator, which decreases a value by 1). So, instead of using the nonexistent operator in Ruby, we would have to rewrite our code so that it looks like this:

```
while counter <= 3
  puts counter
  counter += 1
end
```

This would output the following:

```
1
2
3
=> nil
```

The while statement has a very similar structure to the if statement, but instead of just executing a line of code, the while statement evaluates the condition and will execute the code if the condition is still met.

In this case, before entering the cycle, the counter variable has a value of 1 – as the condition to continue the cycle is for the value to be less than or equal to 3, the condition is met. Since the condition is met, Ruby will execute the code that is before the end keyword, so the number 1 will be printed and a 1 will be added to the counter variable. Since this is a cycle, Ruby will go back and read the condition again, but this time, counter has a value of 2, so it will execute the whole block again. Once the value of the counter reaches 4, Ruby will determine that the while condition is no longer met and break the loop without executing the code inside it again.

A more useful example of loops is when we work with arrays. We already saw one way to iterate through arrays with a counter, but we also have a method called each to iterate through every element of an array. Let's take the instruments_played array again:

```
instruments_played = ["guitar", "drums", "bass", "ukulele"]
```

We can use `each` to go through each element, like this:

```ruby
instruments_played.each do |instrument|
puts instrument
end
```

This code will loop through the array so that we don't have to repeat code for every element of said array. And this is exactly what loops are for: to write less code. For every element in the array, Ruby will print the value of the element (we called it `instrument` for readability, and just for this example, but we can call it anything we want).

Additionally, we can compress this code into a single line by using curly brackets, like so:

```ruby
instruments_played.each { |instrument| puts instrument  }
```

This will have the same output as the previous example, but as you can see, it's more concise and it's quite readable. Additionally, the `each` loop helps us write code that will adapt to the size of the contents. Should we add another element to the array, we would not have to modify anything within our loop to print the added instrument. The loop would do so automatically.

Lastly, what happens when we want to access the index of an array? We have a method just for that. The `each_with_index` method will make the index of the array available, as you can see in this example:

```ruby
instruments_played.each_with_index do |instrument, index|
puts "#{index}: #{instrument}"
end
```

This code will output the following:

```
0: guitar
1: drums
2: bass
3: ukulele
=> ["guitar", "drums", "bass", "ukulele"]
```

Again, both `instrument` and `index` are just aliases – we can name them anything we choose – but the order in which we type them is what will decide which value will be stored in them. The array element value will be stored in the first variable (`instrument`) and the array counter will be stored in the second variable (`index`).

We could very well rewrite the example, like so, and still get the same output:

```ruby
instruments_played.each_with_index do |array_element, array_index|
puts "#{array_index}: #{array_element}"
end
```

The new code will have the same output as before, but this time, we renamed `instrument` and its index to `array_element` and `array_index`, which at this point was just a personal choice I made to make the code make more sense to me. This goes to show that, as programmers, we decide how to name variables in the defense of readability (trust me – the more you grow as a programmer, the more time you'll spend trying to name variables).

At this point, we know how to repeat code by using loops and by iterating through arrays. Instead of writing the same code multiple times, we exploited Ruby's `while` statement and the `each` method to improve efficiency and readability within our code. But we are not done yet. Ruby has a few more tricks up its sleeve to further improve readability. We'll take a look at these tricks in the next section.

Using Ruby language enhancements

For the most part, as developers, we should always strive to increase the readability of our code as this will help everyone in the long run. I've been in scenarios where I've looked back at my code and had trouble understanding what the code was doing. That meant that my code was poorly written. Imagine the toll that this poorly written code may have on the next developer or team that has to use it or, worse, improve it. In contrast, if my code was well written, we wouldn't have this issue. This is me saying this: please write readable code, and I can't stress enough the lengths Ruby developers will go to make their code readable over any other enhancement in our code. Ruby comes with some additional tools to achieve this.

The unless sentence

One example of these options is a language enhancement called the `unless` sentence. The `unless` sentence is a negative `if` sentence – that is, it will execute the code only when the condition is *not* met. Let's see it being used in an example.

Let's assume the following scenario: we have a product aimed at unmarried individuals. For simplicity, we will just print out the message "Promo for singles" if the person is not married. Let's try to write the code for that. Let's take our previous hash example for a person's details:

```
person = { "name" => "Oscar", "age" => 35, "is_married" => true,
"books_read_this_week" => 2.5 }
```

Now, let's change the `is_married` value to `false`:

```
person = { "name" => "Oscar", "age" => 35, "is_married" => false,
"books_read_this_week" => 2.5 }
```

Once we have declared that hash, we can try to print a message if the person is single:

```
puts "Promo for singles" if person["is_married"] == false
```

Because the person is not married, the output is as follows:

```
Promo for singles
```

And while the code works, it simply doesn't look good. We could use the bang (!) operator to invert the Boolean value from true to false:

```
puts "Show promotion" if !person["is_married"]
```

Though this code still works, it still looks bad. Let's look at the options Ruby has to fix this.

In most programming languages, you'll see a lot of sentences that read "if not." Of course, this is awful to read and goes against the readability principles of Ruby. To solve this issue, Ruby's creators added the exact sentence to make this more readable: unless. It works similarly to the if statement but will execute the code if the condition is deemed false.

In this case, this is helpful when we have code to be executed only when the person is not married. So, instead of writing an if negative sentence (if a person is *not* married), if !person["is_married"], we could rewrite the example as follows (unless a person is married):

```
unless person["is_married"]
  puts "Show promotion"
end
```

This is looking much better already, but just like the if statement, we can convert it into a one-liner:

```
puts "Show promotion" unless person["is_married"]
```

This is a very Ruby-esque sentence, reading exactly like it behaves: "Print "Show promotion" unless the person is married." This is about as readable as it gets.

The unless sentence is so useful that one of the most used PHP frameworks today, called Laravel, has borrowed this functionality in the form of a directive: https://laravel.com/docs/9.x/blade#if-statements.

The until loop

Just like the unless sentence, the until loop solves the same issue with negative conditions.

Instead of writing "while not," which reads horribly, the until sentence takes a false statement and executes the loop until the condition becomes true.

The until sentence takes a false statement and executes the loop until the condition becomes true. Let's look at our while example from earlier again:

```
counter = 1
while counter <= 3
```

```
  puts counter
  counter += 1
end
```

Using `until`, we can rewrite it as follows:

```
counter = 1
until counter > 3
  puts counter
  counter += 1
end
```

The output is the same as with the `while` statement:

```
1
2
3
=> nil
```

Our code would read like "Print the counter until the counter is larger than 3." Whether you choose to use the `while not` sentence or the `until` sentence will be up to you as they both seem readable, but the fact that Ruby has both sentences available tells us that Ruby is designed to be read and not just programmed.

Automatic returns

When working within the IRB, you may have noticed that whenever you type variables, the IRB will output the value you just typed. Even on our last `until` statement example, the shell first outputs the three numbers and then a final `=> nil` value. If you take a closer look at the other examples, you'll see a similar behavior. This is because Ruby always attempts to return a value – be it a declaration, a method, or just a string, Ruby will try to automatically return a value.

If you're not convinced, let's use the IRB to see it more explicitly. So, type the following:

```
"This is a string"
```

We are not declaring the string or assigning it to a value; we are simply typing a string into the IRB shell. And what does the shell do? It returns the value we just typed:

```
=> "this is a string"
```

Coming from a PHP background (and other languages for that matter), grasping the "automatic return" feature is crucial to understanding more complex Ruby code. It's important to know that PHP (and most languages) do not behave this way. PHP (and other languages) require us to explicitly return the value, while Ruby does this by default. In PHP, this is achieved by using the `return` sentence.

That said, from time to time, you will encounter Ruby code with an explicit `return` statement, as it will sometimes increase readability. To further understand this feature, for the next few examples, we'll exit the IRB and continue by creating source code files and running Ruby to execute them. You may still follow the next examples in the IRB, but I would highly recommend that you follow them with source code files instead of the IRB.

Let's say we wanted to create a method that prints a message on the screen. We can do so by creating a file called `methods.rb`. This file will contain the following code:

```
# methods.rb
def message()
  return "This is a message"
end
```

For now, we're defining a method called `message` that returns a string. In Ruby, we define a method with the `def` reserved keyword and limit the definition with the `end` keyword.

Now, let's add another method called `say()` and, inside that method, call the `message()` method:

```
# methods.rb
...
def say()
  message()
end
```

So far, we haven't done anything out of the ordinary – we just have one method calling another. If we opened a shell and executed this script, it would appear to be doing nothing:

```
ruby methods.rb
```

This script outputs nothing, but behind the scenes, it has two methods that are now defined and ready to be used. The `message` method is explicitly (not automatically) returning a string because of the use of the `return` keyword. This code still looks familiar, but not for long.

Now, let's print out the contents of the `say()` method with this last line on the code:

```
# methods.rb
...
def say()
  return message()
end
puts say()
```

If we run this again, we will see the following message on the screen:

```
This is a message
```

And this is where Ruby behaves differently to PHP. While you can explicitly use the `return` function in Ruby, Ruby does not need the `return` statement because it already does it automatically as part of its default behavior. So let's try it out by removing the return statement from both the `message()` and the `say()` methods. Your final code should look like this:

```
# methods.rb
def message()
  "This is a message"
end
def say()
  message()
end
puts say()
```

Admittedly, this looks weird, especially for someone from a PHP background. My advice to you is to just try to get used to this syntax. You'll see it very often in Ruby. To make it easier to learn this rule, we can generalize and say, "Every sentence in Ruby will return a value." With some notable exceptions, this is true for all Ruby sentences.

Optional parentheses

Another weird but useful syntactic enhancement is that the parentheses on Ruby methods are purely optional – so, you can choose whether to include parentheses or not. And just like every Ruby resource we've learned about so far, we should try to use it to make our code easier to read, but we should also try to avoid overusing it. Excessive use of this feature could have us formatting our code like this:

```
method1 method2 parmeter1, parameter2
```

The problem with this snippet is that we don't know if the comma is being used for separating the arguments for `method1` or `method2`. In this case, we should use parenthesis:

```
method1( method2( parameter1, parameter2 )
```

Now, it's more than clear that `method2` is receiving two arguments while `method1` is just receiving one argument. Let's look at a more simplified example by removing the parenthesis from our previous examples. Our example will now look like this:

```
# methods.rb
def message
  "This is a message"
end
```

```
def say
  puts message
end

say
```

The output is the same as before, but now, the code looks a lot more like proper sentences instead of code syntax. You'll see a lot of code similar to this, especially when you start using Ruby on Rails. Because of the lack of parenthesis, Ruby allows us to have a method and a variable with the same name. In this case, we have a method called message and a variable called message.

This scenario, if left unexplained, can lead to a lot of confusion later on. To that effect, let's take our previous example and tweak it so that we have a better understanding of this naming behavior. First, we'll add a parameter to the say() method so that the printed message is dynamic. This parameter will be named message:

```
# methods.rb
...
def say message
  puts message
end
say "Now we can say anything"
```

In other programming languages, we would expect an error if we tried to run this code, and this is where Ruby can sometimes be overwhelming when you're starting to use it. We purposely named the parameter message, which means we now have a message method and a message local variable. When reaching the puts message line, we are not sure if we are calling the message parameter or the message method without the parentheses. Unfortunately, this confusion happens more often than not, or at least that was my experience when I started to use Ruby more professionally.

So, my advice here is to try to use parenthesis when calling methods, even when the syntax doesn't require us to use them. For teaching purposes, we won't be doing it in this example. So, our final source code should look like this:

```
# methods.rb

def message
  return "This is a message"
end

def say message
  puts message
end

say "Now we can say anything"
```

As you would expect (or not), when executing the script on the shell, we'll get the following output:

```
Now we can say anything
```

Why did it print that string and not the `"This is a message"` string? Well, this is because the `message` variable took precedence over the `message` method.

While this feature may not seem pretty (I don't like it that much), I guarantee you that you'll come across it from time to time, and you should be prepared for it.

Questionable exclamation method names

As a cherry on top of the language enhancements in Ruby, its creators have also included a naming feature to add readability to our methods: the exclamation mark (`!`) (also known as a bang) and the question mark (`?`). They don't change behavior in any way, but they allow for a line of code to read as a question or as an exclamation. Methods named with the exclamation mark are called dangerous methods because they modify the object from where they are called. Methods named with the question mark are called predicate methods and, by convention, return a Boolean.

To see this in action, we'll create a method with the question mark. Let's create a new file called `enhanced_naming.rb` and add the following code:

```
# enhanced_naming.rb
$married_status = false

def is_married
  $married_status
end
```

The `$married_status` variable is a global variable, which simply means that we can modify or access its contents on a method or outside the method. In this case, we defined a method that gets the `$married_status` value. However, knowing that we can add the `?` to the name of this method, let's rename the `is_married` method like so:

```
# enhanced_naming.rb
$married_status = false

def is_married?
  $married_status
end
```

Now, let's use an already familiar one-liner to print a message for a married person:

```
puts "Promo for married people" if is_married?
```

While adding ? to the name of the method does not affect its behavior, it does change the sentence into an obvious question. We'll see this syntax very often in Ruby.

Similarly, we can use the bang symbol (!) as part of the name of a method. Again, adding it to the name doesn't affect the behavior by itself, but it tells whoever is reading the code that we're doing something different than just calling a method. As an example, let's rename our `marry` method to `marry!` and see what it looks like:

```ruby
def marry!
  $married_status = true
end
```

As a convention adopted by the Ruby community, the bang symbol (!) will tell the reader (of the code) that we are making a change within an object. A method without the bang symbol would simply return a value, but not affect the object itself. So, in this case, we are changing the `$married_status` value to `true`. This is what the code should look like now:

```ruby
# enhanced_naming.rb

$married_status = false

def is_married?
  $married_status
end

def marry!
  $married_status = true
end

puts "Promo for married people" if is_married?
```

Sadly, when we run this example, we don't see any output. This is because the initial value of the global `$married_status` variable is `false`, and our code will only print a message if the value is `true`. Now, let's call the `marry!` method and copy the one-liner again at the end of the code:

```ruby
puts "Promo for married people" if is_married?
marry!
puts "Promo for married people" if is_married?
```

Now, we can run the code again:

```ruby
ruby enhanced.rb
```

The output will look like this:

```
Promo for married people
```

What's happening here? We have a global $married_status variable with an initial false value. Then, we have two methods – one to get the $married_status value and another to change it to true. Finally, we attempt to print the message but since the initial value is false, the message is not printed. By calling the marry! method, we change $married_status to true, which makes the last line of our script print out the message.

Ruby brings language enhancements to programming merely to improve code readability. I've seen code written so beautifully that it reinforces the idea behind not writing comments on your code, but rather lets your code speak for itself. Once you start using them regularly, you will appreciate them more and more and you'll wish all languages had these enhancements.

Summary

In this chapter, we learned how to write, execute, and require scripts with the Ruby binary, along with how to use the IRB to execute Ruby code directly on the command line without having to write source code.

Additionally, we reviewed Ruby's syntax for writing variables, the syntax for if statements, and how to loop through both cycles and arrays. Finally, we learned some of the language enhancements that Ruby has and PHP doesn't so that we can read and understand more complex Ruby code.

Now, we are ready to write Ruby code to solve real-life examples. We'll start doing this in the next chapter.

4

Ruby Scripting versus PHP Scripting

Just like the similarities we found when we looked at Ruby's and PHP's syntax, we are going to take things a step further and dive into the similarities between Ruby scripts and PHP scripts. A script is a piece of code that will run a task and then stop its execution. Said task may be simple or complex, but it is not considered an application as it stops once the task is done and only performs the task. Let's take this step together and start writing simple scripts so that we can eventually write full-fledged applications.

With that in mind, in this chapter, we will cover the following topics:

- Useful scripts
- Text handling
- File handling
- Command-line arguments

Technical requirements

To follow along with this chapter, we will need the following:

- Any IDE to view/edit code (for example, SublimeText, Visual Studio Code, Notepad++ Vim, Emacs, and so on)
- For macOS users, you will also need to have XCode Command Line Tools installed
- Ruby version 2.6 or later must be installed and ready to use

The code presented in this chapter is available at `https://github.com/PacktPublishing/From-PHP-to-Ruby-on-Rails/`.

Beyond Hello World

In the previous chapter, we learned how to run (or execute) Ruby code. However, we only focused on the syntax and not the usefulness of the code. The famous Hello World script we write in any language is, by itself, useless, at least from a practical sense. So, let's start learning how to use some tools to give our scripts a little bit of usefulness.

One useful tool in any language is having a way to verify the version of the programming language that we are currently using. Once we obtain the version, we can stop the execution if the version we are using is incorrect. So, our first step is to get the current Ruby version. Let's create a file called `version_verification.rb` with the following code:

```
# version_verification.rb
puts "We are running Ruby version #{RUBY_VERSION}"
```

We can run this script on our shell by typing the following command:

```
ruby version_verifications.rb
```

It should output something similar to this:

```
We are running Ruby version 2.6.8
```

In this script, we are using the RUBY_VERSION constant to get the current version of Ruby that we are using and interpolating this constant with a string to view the whole message regarding the Ruby version. By itself, this constant is useless, but let's give it some practical use. Let's say we wanted to share our script with other teams, where it would be used in different computers and/or environments. To make sure our script works properly, we would have to provide certain requirements or conditions for our script. It would be also useful to verify that said requirements are being met. We have a couple of options to accomplish this. We could simply compare the version we obtain from the RUBY_VERSION constant to another string, such as '2.6.8'. That would be the most straightforward way to do this. However, the problem with this approach is that you would have to have the same Ruby version everywhere and that is rarely the case. We almost always have small variations of the version. If we were to take the preceding example of '2.6.8', in other systems, we could get '2.6.5', '2.6.7', or even '2.6.9'. And all of these versions would not only be equivalent but also valid to what we are requiring. So, let's just say our requirement is 2.6 and above, which would be equivalent to any version above '2.5.9'. We could split the obtained version from the RUBY_VERSION constant, split its value by the dots, and start comparing away. However, this is too much work; this is where comes Ruby to the rescue. Ruby comes with a library called `stdlib` that comes with several utilities that are extremely useful when encountering these types of problems. Specifically, Ruby has the `Gem::Version` class, which will solve our problem at hand. We'll include it in our example, but to make sure that the validation works, we will compare it to version `'3.0'`. Once we've tested the validation, we can add the correct version (`'2.6'`). Our code now looks like this:

```
# version_verification.rb
puts "Incompatible Ruby version" if Gem::Version.new(RUBY_VERSION) <
Gem::Version.new('3.0')
puts "We are running Ruby version #{RUBY_VERSION}"
```

If we were to run this script on our shell, we would get the following output:

```
Incompatible Ruby version
We are running Ruby version 2.6.8
```

Our validation worked, but the problem now is that we are not stopping the execution if we don't have the correct Ruby version. The message showing the Ruby version should not be shown. If we were writing our script in PHP, we could simply use the `die()` function (which is equivalent to the `exit()` language construct) and the script would stop then and there. However, since we are writing scripts, certain practices can make our script even more useful. If our program was running on the web, we would rely on HTTP response status codes (`https://developer.mozilla.org/en-US/docs/Web/HTTP/Status`) to tell the browser that our page was rendered and an error occurred. Similarly, in scripts, we rely on exit codes (`https://www.baeldung.com/linux/status-codes`) to tell the shell that our program failed. Taking that into account, we would then use the `Kernel::exit()` method to both stop the execution and send the shell a signal that our script failed. This method receives an argument that is then sent to the shell. This argument is an error code that can be used by the operating system. We will be using error code 1 as it refers to a general error. After making this adjustment, our code would now look like this:

```
# version_verification.rb
Kernel::exit(1) if Gem::Version.new(RUBY_VERSION) < Gem::Version.
new('3.0')
puts "We are running Ruby version #{RUBY_VERSION}"
```

If we run this script on the shell, there would be no output as the script stops the execution before the message. In Unix-based systems, right after our script stops, we can run the following:

```
echo $?
```

This would return 1, which is the same as the argument we passed to the `exit()` method. `$?` returns the exit code of the last command that was run.

> **Note for Windows users**
>
> For Windows users, the shell will have a different output, depending on what Windows shell you use. If you're using Powershell, you could obtain the same output by executing the `echo $LastExitCode` command in PowerShell.

Refer to the Windows documentation for more information regarding this variable: `https://learn.microsoft.com/en-us/powershell/module/microsoft.powershell.core/about/about_automatic_variables?view=powershell-7.3`.

There is still one last tweak we need for our Ruby version verification script to be complete. As I mentioned previously, we only added version `'3.0'` to make sure our code worked, but in reality, we want to verify that our installed version is greater than `'2.6'`. So, our final verification will look like this:

```
# version_verification.rb
Kernel::exit(1) if Gem::Version.new(RUBY_VERSION) > Gem::Version.
new('2.6')
puts "We are running Ruby version #{RUBY_VERSION}"
```

If we executed our script on the shell, we would get the following:

We are running Ruby version 2.6.8

And with that, we have made sure that if our script is executed with a Ruby version lower than `'2.6'` (for example, `'2.5.7'` or `'2.2.1'`), then the script will stop and send an error signal. Congratulations! We've created our first useful piece of code. This technique is often used by seasoned Ruby developers who are very aware of version changes. It will be up to you to improve this snippet as you could add an error message and also add an upper limit (for example, greater than `'2.5.9'` but lower than `'3.0'`). Now that we've created our first truly useful script, let's take a look at some other useful Ruby tools for handling text.

Text handling

You will most likely encounter strings (texts) in your journey to becoming a Ruby developer, so it's important to know how to handle and manipulate this type of data. Whether you need to capitalize, get a partial string, or even trim a string, Ruby comes with a vast arsenal of tools to manipulate text as we see fit. Most programming languages have this type of tool, and Ruby is not an exception. As an example, let's say we wanted to grab a previously entered name and make sure that all the letters were in uppercase or lowercase. Ruby has two methods to do exactly that: `upcase()` and `downcase()`. Let's try them out by creating a file called `string_cases.rb` with the following code:

```
first_name = "benjamin"
last_name = "BECKER"
puts "My full name is #{first_name} #{last_name}"
```

So far, we've declared two variables and used interpolation to output the full name. Let's say we were to run this script on the shell with the following:

```
ruby string_cases.rb
```

The output would be as follows:

```
My full name is benjamin BECKER.
```

The output is nothing unexpected, given that we declared the name with lowercase letters and the last name with uppercase letters. However, it doesn't make sense to have a first name in one case and a last name in another. So, we can either make them both uppercase or both lowercase. Let's try both solutions.

The upcase method

To make them both uppercase, we can use the `upcase()` method. Our code will look as follows:

```
first_name = "benjamin"
last_name = "BECKER"
puts "My full name is #{first_name.upcase} #{last_name}"
```

If we tested this code by running it again on the shell, we would get the following output:

```
My full name is BENJAMIN BECKER.
```

The downcase method

Similarly, we could make all characters lowercase with `downcase()`. In this case, our code would look like this:

```
first_name = "benjamin"
last_name = "BECKER"
puts "My full name is #{first_name} #{last_name.downcase}"
```

So, with this last change, if we ran the script, we would obtain the following output:

```
My full name is benjamin becker
```

As you can see, we can change the variable's case with both `upcase()` and `downcase()`. However, we can also do the same directly to a string and not just a variable. To see that in action, let's change our code to the following:

```
first_name = "benjamin"
last_name = "BECKER"
puts "My full name is #{first_name} #{last_name}".upcase
```

This time, we took the whole output string and changed it to uppercase. The output will be as follows:

```
MY FULL NAME IS BENJAMIN BECKER
```

And while this is fun and all, it's only useful for learning purposes. So, let's add some usefulness to our script with an additional method. For users, reading the full name in either all uppercase or all lowercase will not make sense and certainly not look professional. So, let's capitalize only the first letter of both the `first_name` and `last_name` variables.

The capitalize method

We can do this with the `capitalize()` method. Now, our code will look like this:

```
first_name = "benjamin"
last_name = "BECKER"
puts "My full name is #{first_name.capitalize} #{last_name.
capitalize}"
```

If we run this example, the output on the shell will look like this:

```
My full name is Benjamin Becker
```

Note that Ruby "knows" what characters to make uppercase and what characters to make lowercase to get this "capitalized" output. Ruby has many other methods to handle and manipulate text. We could spend the rest of this chapter looking at many of these methods, but I'd like to focus more on other tools and challenge you to check out the text methods for yourself. The documentation for these methods is pretty clear, and it helps that these methods were built using the Ruby philosophy and best practices. I recommend that you take a look at the `strip`, `lstrip`, `rstrip`, `start_with?`, `end_with?`, `rindex`, `gsub`, `chomp`, and `chop` methods:

- `https://apidock.com/ruby/String/strip`
- `https://apidock.com/ruby/String/lstrip`
- `https://apidock.com/ruby/String/rstrip`
- `https://apidock.com/ruby/String/start_with%3F`
- `https://apidock.com/ruby/String/end_with%3F`
- `https://apidock.com/ruby/String/rindex`
- `https://apidock.com/ruby/String/gsub`
- `https://apidock.com/ruby/String/chomp`
- `https://apidock.com/ruby/String/chop`

You might be more familiar with the names of these methods as PHP has similar methods as the ones I just mentioned: `trim`, `ltrim`, `rtrim`, `str_starts_with`, `str_ends_with`, `strpos`, and `str_replace`. The `chomp` and `chop` methods are very different in PHP, so I suggest that you take a close look at them in Ruby as they can be extremely useful.

The ease of use and usefulness of the aforementioned methods are proof of why we should rely on Ruby's string methods to do our string manipulation. We could certainly write all of this functionality on our own, but that would be just reinventing the wheel and we would be wasting time and energy. Should you choose to do that, I certainly won't stop you as you would probably learn a lot of Ruby in the process. However, in this guided tour that I'm giving you, we will stick to learning more of the tools that Ruby provides for us. Now, let's look at how Ruby allows us to do another powerful action: handle files.

File manipulation

Some decades ago, one of the few options (if not the only option) for saving information was storing it in files. All sort of data was stored in these files: passwords, user data, config data, and more. Saving information in plain text files was, at the time, the most feasible option to save information. It all came to an end with the advent of **databases (DBs)** and DB usage. DBs became a more feasible and popular option, and they now came in different flavors. While this is still true today, using a DB comes with a quite expensive cost. I'm not only talking about a monetary cost – I'm talking about it in terms of memory, disk, and processing time. So, in certain use cases, it's still a much better option to use plain text files to store information. To that purpose, most programming languages, including Ruby and PHP, make this task straightforward. Let's take a look at how we can take advantage of the file manipulation tooling that comes with Ruby.

Let's suppose we wanted to grab a user's first name from a file. For this, we must create a file. The file will be called name.txt. We could name it without the file extension (.txt) and it would have no impact on the functionality of our script, but it's always a good practice to give hints to our fellow developers as to the intent of our script. It's pretty easy to assume that a file named name.txt will most probably contain text, and that text will be a name. So, let's create the text file and add some text to it:

```
mary
```

Now, let's focus on opening this file. There are different modes when opening files in Ruby, but for now, we will focus on reading data from the file. Let's create a file called reading_file.rb and add the following code to it:

```
# reading_file.rb
File.open("name.txt")
```

First, we have to get Ruby to open the file so that it can handle and manipulate it. The File.open() method does exactly that. But now, we need to fetch the file's contents to be able to use it in our script. First, we will assign the File.open() result to a variable. Our code will look like this:

```
# reading_file.rb
file_instance = File.open("name.txt")
```

With that, we saved the result of the `File.open()` method to the `file_instance` variable, which, in turn, now lets us have access to the file's contents. Ruby has a very intuitive method for grabbing a file's contents: the `read()` method. The `read()` method grabs a file's contents and casts it into a string. So, let's grab that string and output it to make sure our script is working. Now, our script looks like this:

```
# reading_file.rb
file_instance = File.open("name.txt")
user_name = file_instance.read
puts "The user's name is #{user_name}"
```

If we were to run our script on the shell with `ruby reading_file.rb`, the output would be as follows:

The user's name is mary

And voilà – we have successfully read a value from a text file. In the code, we got Ruby to open the `name.txt` file. Then, from the instance we got as a result, we obtained the original file's contents as a string. Lastly, we used the value in a string to output something useful to the user. We can get fancy and capitalize the username with our already acquainted `capitalize()` method. We can also test that our script is reading from the `name.txt` file. Let's open the `name.txt` file and change the name contained in the file to something else:

```
nancy
```

Now, let's run our script in the shell again with `ruby reading_file.rb`. The output should be as follows:

The user's name is nancy

Regarding reading a file's contents, this is as easy as it gets. The code, while not as intuitive as other examples we've written, is still simple and readable. Now, let's write another example in which we could include the user's last name. We could simply add the last name to the text file, and it would be a valid solution, but let's look at that solution and a couple of variations. So, let's add a new text file called `full_name.txt` with the following content:

```
paul smith
```

We're going to manipulate this file with another Ruby script called `full_name.rb`. Initially, the script is going to be the same as the `reading_file.rb` script. We can even just copy the file, but we are going to make some tweaks to separate the full name into `name` and `last_name`. We'll also change the `name.txt` parameter to `full_name.txt`. So, let's look at the code in the `full_name.rb` file:

```
# full_name.rb
file_instance = File.open("full_name.txt")
```

```
user_name = file_instance.read
puts "The user's name is #{user_name}"
```

If we execute this script on the shell with `ruby full_name.rb`, the output will be as follows:

The user's name is paul smith

There's nothing unexpected here as the functionality is pretty much the same as the first script, `reading_file.rb`. But what if we wanted to have the name and the last name capitalized? We could try using the `capitalize()` method on the `user_name` variable. Let's do that. The line where we output `user_name` will look like this:

```
puts "The user's name is #{user_name.capitalize}"
```

However, when we run the script again, the output will be as follows:

The user's name is Paul smith

Unfortunately for us, the `capitalize()` method only changes the first letter of the first word to uppercase. But do not despair, as we can accomplish the correct upper casing with just a single line of code. Before we do that, we will look at three additional methods: `split()`, `map()`, and `join()`.

The split() method

We can use `split()` to divide a word by spaces into an array. Simply put, `split()` would turn `paul smith` into an array of `[ "paul", "smith" ]`, which we can use in our current situation. So, let's incorporate it into our code:

```
# full_name.rb
file_instance = File.open("full_name.txt")
user_name = file_instance.read.split
puts "The user's name is #{user_name[0]} #{user_name[1]}"
```

In the preceding code, we took the string from the file and applied the `split()` method.

This method divided the `paul smith` into an array of two elements. In the end, we used the element on the 0 slot (`user_name[0]`) and the 1 slot (`user_name[0]`) and embedded them into the string. For now, the output is the same, but with the advantage that we have divided the name into two words. We could apply the `capitalize()` method to both elements and be done with our task at hand. But this is when we have to take a step back and think in more broad terms for our script. What would happen if someone had a middle name? Or how would our script behave if a user had two last names? Our script would truncate part of the name in both of these cases. It is our job, as developers, to create code that is generic and that will behave properly, even with some unexpected input. This is where the `map()` method proves useful.

The map() method

The map() method is equivalent to iterating through an array and applying a method to each element of the array in a single line. It receives a method that we want to apply to each element as a parameter. So, let's have another rewrite of our script:

```
# full_name.rb
file_instance = File.open("full_name.txt")
user_name = file_instance.read.split.map(&:capitalize)
puts "The user's name is #{user_name}"
```

Now, the output is something slightly strange, but closer to what we're looking for. If we run this script again, we will get the following output:

```
The user's name is ["Paul", "Smith"]
```

We are almost there. Here, we are reading the name from the file, then dividing it by spaces into words, and finally applying each word to the capitalize() method. The problem with the output is that, yes, we've capitalized each element of the array, but then we are printing the whole array as a string, so the square brackets (' [ ] ') are included on the string. We are missing one last step, which is where the join() method comes in handy.

The join() method

The join() method does the opposite of split(). The join() method takes an array, converts it into a string, and glues each element with what we set as a parameter. So, the last step is to make the user_name array a string, each element separated by a white space. So, let's add that last touch:

```
# full_name.rb
file_instance = File.open("full_name.txt")
user_name = file_instance.read.split.map(&:capitalize).join(' ')
puts "The user's name is #{user_name}"
```

And with that, our generic script is done. Let's take it out for a ride. If we were to run it on the shell, the output would be as follows:

```
The user's name is Paul Smith
```

Now, since we claim that our script is generic, it should not be an issue if we were to add a middle name. So, let's change the name in the full_name.txt file:

```
paul isaac smith
```

If we were to run the script again, the output would be as follows:

```
The user's name is Paul Isaac Smith
```

We are still missing the other use case that I mentioned in which some people in some countries have two last names. So, let's change the name one more time in our full_name.txt file:

```
benjamin eliseo pineda avendaño
```

As with the other examples, the script will run correctly and output the following:

```
The user's name is Benjamin Eliseo Pineda Avendaño
```

We've successfully made a truly generic piece of code. It will work whether we add a single name, a generic name (name and last name), or a special combination of first, middle, and two last names. While the code is not as readable as other snippets we've read, I can guarantee that you will encounter a combination of the split(), map(), and join() methods whenever you move into more advanced code. Once we get to using the Ruby on Rails framework, you will see and use both of these methods there.

So far, we've only written code in read-only mode. Now, let's look at creating and modifying file contents.

Creating and modifying file contents

One practical use of reading and writing a file would be creating and modifying a counter value saved in a text file. What if we wanted to keep track of how many times a script has been executed? We could add a file with a number and each time we run the script, we could increment this value and simply output it to the user. We'll start by creating a file called counter.rb with the following code:

```
# counter.rb
file_instance = File.open("counter.txt", "w")
counter = file_instance.read
puts "Time(s) script has been run: #{counter}"
```

Again, we are opening a file, but in this case, we've added an additional parameter ("w") so that we can write contents to the file. Additionally, we are going to try to create the file with our script instead of creating it by ourselves. So, let's run this script from the shell with ruby counter.rb. The output should be as follows:

```
counter.rb:3:in 'read': not opened for reading (IOError)
        from counter.rb:3:in '<main>'
```

Unfortunately for us, this is an error. If we look closer at the error description, it reads not opened for reading. This is because we set "w" mode, which is a write-only mode. We can only write to the file in this mode. However, we need to both read and write the contents of the file. Also, notice that the counter.txt file has been created, and that's an advantage of "w" mode. If the file we are trying to write doesn't exist, it will create it for us. We want this behavior, but we also want to be able to read the contents of the file. So, let's change the mode to "a+" in our script:

```
# counter.rb
file_instance = File.open("counter.txt", "a+")
counter = file_instance.read
puts "Time(s) script has been run: #{counter}"
```

Don't forget to delete the counter.txt file and execute the script again. The output will now look like this:

```
Time(s) script has been run:
```

If we check the folder in which our script is, we will notice that the counter.txt file has been created. However, the value is empty, which is unintended. So, let's tweak our script to convert that into a number:

```
# counter.rb
file_instance = File.open("counter.txt", "a+")
counter = file_instance.read.to_i
puts "Time(s) script has been run: #{counter}"
```

Notice that on line 3 of our script, we've added .to_i at the end of the line, which converts the contents of the string into a number. In this scenario, the file is empty and thus returns an empty string, which, in turn, is converted into a 0. Let's run this script again. The output will be as follows:

```
Time(s) script has been run: 0
```

So far, so good. However, if we run it again, the output will remain the same as we have not added the functionality to increment the number. Let's do just that:

```
# counter.rb
file_instance = File.open("counter.txt", "a+")
counter = file_instance.read.to_i
puts "Time(s) script has been run: #{counter}"
counter += 1
File.write("counter.txt", counter)
```

With the last two lines, we've incremented the counter value by one and written the said value to the same `counter.txt` file. As a final test for this script, let's delete the `counter.txt` file once more and run the script a few times. This should be the output:

```
Time(s) script has been run: 0
Time(s) script has been run: 1
Time(s) script has been run: 2
Time(s) script has been run: 3
```

With this output, we can confirm that our script has run correctly a couple of times. As I mentioned previously, even with the existence of DBs, file reading and writing can be useful, be it for saving configuration values or for logging, and it is fast and easy to implement. You can find additional examples and modes at `https://www.rubyguides.com/2015/05/working-with-files-ruby/`.

Now that we've established how we can read and write to and from files, let's take a look at the next feature that will help us give our scripts more usefulness: command-line arguments.

Command-line arguments

So far, we've added both variable and fixed (either numeric or string) values to our code. To make our scripts more generic and more usable for other folks, we can add parameters that won't be hardcoded within the code. If you're not familiar with the term, *hardcoded* is the practice of writing fixed variable values within code. In our previous examples, we added the filename that we were going to open as a fixed value – that is, to change it, we would have to change the source code. To avoid that, we could pass the script a value (a filename, in this case) that whoever runs the script can change. Passing values to a script is what we commonly refer to as command-line arguments. We can have multiple arguments, a single argument, or as we've done so far, no arguments. Let's start with a simple example, then work our way up to more complex examples that will help us make our scripts more generic.

Let's start by taking a string as a command-line argument on a script, format it, and output it to the shell. We will start by creating a script called `command_line.rb` with the following code:

```
# command_line.rb
input_arguments = ARGV
puts "Hello #{input_arguments[0]}"
```

In this script, we are using `ARGV`, which is an array that contains any parameters passed to our script, then assigns it to a variable, to finally pass its first value to a string to be outputted. Let's try running the script. First, let's try it with no arguments by running this on the shell:

```
ruby command_line.rb
```

This will output the following:

```
Hello
```

We received this output we have not passed any command-line arguments to our script. So, how do we pass arguments, you may ask? Well, it's as simple as writing the value right after the filename when we run it. Now, let's try this with a name value. On the shell, run the following:

```
ruby command_line.rb marco
```

We will now see the following output:

```
Hello marco
```

As we can see, Ruby detects a single value on the ARGV array, and as a result, the output shows the same value we passed to the script. Unlike the value we obtained through opening a file, the ARGV array works a bit differently. Let's try adding a second argument to our script. Let's run it with both a different name and a second parameter. Back in the shell, run the following:

```
ruby command_line.rb ben franco
```

The output will be as follows:

```
Hello ben
```

This is because we are only using the first value of the input_arguments array – that is, the value contained in input_arguments[0]. Ruby takes the string that is passed as an argument, automatically splits it by spaces, and then places each element in the ARGV array. Let's use all of the arguments that are being passed and wrap up this example. We will take the map() and join() combo that we previously used in the file handling examples to glue and show all arguments passed to the script, and since it's a name, we will capitalize it in the process. So, let's tweak our script once more so that it does just that:

```
# command_line.rb
input_arguments = ARGV
puts "Hello #{input_arguments.map(&:capitalize).join(' ')}"
```

Now, let's run it a couple of times with different names each time:

```
ruby command_line.rb ben aaron jones
```

This will output the following:

```
Hello Ben Aaron Jones
```

Let's try it with more parameters:

```
ruby command_line.rb gaby audra luna WOODHOUSE
```

This will output the following:

```
Hello Gaby Audra Luna Woodhouse
```

The same goes for running it with fewer arguments. Let's give this one more try with a single name:

```
ruby command_line.rb al
```

This will also run but with a single name, just like on the first iteration of the script. The output will be as follows:

```
Hello Al
```

Now that we understand the basics of command-line arguments, let's start giving them a bit more usefulness. Let's write a script that will take two arguments, the first being a name and the second being a digit. We will get our script to get the digit and print the name as many times as that digit. We will also add an error message if the script is run with fewer or more arguments than what we need for our script to work. So, let's start by creating a file called `validate_arguments.rb` and add the following code to it:

```
# validate_arguments.rb
input_arguments = ARGV
name = input_arguments.first
cycle_times = input_arguments.last.to_i
cycle_times.times { puts name }
```

In this script, we get the command-line arguments and use the first one as the name and the last one as the counter for our cycle. With the `cycle_times` variable, we're casting (or converting) the value of the last element of the `input_arguments` array from a string into an integer. Then, we're using the `times` method to repeat a piece of code inside the curly brackets. Now, let's try running our script with the following values:

```
ruby validate_arguments.rb gabriela 5
```

As expected, the output of the script is as follows:

```
gabriela
gabriela
gabriela
gabriela
gabriela
```

We may think our work here is done, but we'd be wrong. This is what we call the *happy path*, in which we feed our script values that the script is expecting and thus the script's behavior is correct. However, this is utopic as this never happens in real life. In real life, the user will forget to feed the script both parameters or will feed the parameters in the wrong order. We, as coders, need to take this into account and code appropriately. We need to validate that the input we feed the script is either correct or that we need to tell the user that the parameters are incorrect. What happens if we invert the parameters? Let's see:

```
ruby validate_arguments.rb 5 gabriela
```

This outputs nothing. Let's try running the script with no arguments:

```
ruby validate_arguments.rb
```

This also outputs nothing. This is a mistake on our side because we know how our script works, but someone who might be using the script doesn't. There is no documentation and the least we can do is output error messages that can guide the user as to the correct usage of the script. Additionally, we have to assume that the end user does not know how to program and is not going to open the script to view its usage. So, let's start by validating that the script only receives two arguments. Also, let's add an error message to help the user out. Let's create our validation in our code. Our `validate_arguments. rb` script will now look like this:

```
# validate_arguments.rb
if ARGV.size != 2
  puts "Error. The script has failed!"
end
input_arguments = ARGV
name = input_arguments.first
cycle_times = input_arguments.last.to_i
cycle_times.times { puts name }
```

Now, when we run it again without any arguments, we will see an error message:

```
Error. The script has failed!
```

However, even though we are seeing an error, the script is still going through the whole code, which is not what we want. To prove this, let's add another message at the end of the code:

```
# validate_arguments.rb
if ARGV.size != 2
  puts "Error. The script has failed!"
end
input_arguments = ARGV
name = input_arguments.first
cycle_times = input_arguments.last.to_i
```

```
cycle_times.times { puts name }
puts "But we are still running the script"
```

Let's run the script again (with no arguments):

```
ruby validate_arguments.rb
```

The output will be as follows:

```
Error. The script has failed!
But we are still running the script.
```

As we learned previously, we need to stop the execution of the script once we've figured out that we have errors. So, let's fix this and stop the execution with a `Kernel::exit()` call. Let's also add a suggestion to fix the problem:

```
# validate_arguments.rb
if ARGV.size != 2
  puts "Error. The script has failed!"
  puts "Usage: ruby validate_arguments.rb name times_to_repeat"
  Kernel::exit(1)
end
input_arguments = ARGV
name = input_arguments.first
cycle_times = input_arguments.last.to_i
cycle_times.times { puts name }
puts "But we are still running the script"
```

Let's run the script once again without arguments:

```
ruby validate_arguments.rb
```

This time, we will get the correct output, and the execution will be stopped at the right point:

```
Error. The script has failed!
Usage: ruby validate_arguments.rb name times_to_repeat
```

As you can see, we are no longer outputting the `But we are still running the script.` message. This is because once the script does not pass the validation block, its execution is stopped. This is great progress for our script. However, we are still missing one piece of validation. In previous examples, we inverted the arguments by passing the number and then the name. Even with our tweaks and validations, this is a use case that will still make our script behave erroneously. Let's try it out:

```
ruby validate_arguments.rb 3 henry
```

This will output the following:

```
We are still running the script.
```

Again, we have no information as to why the output is empty, which can be very frustrating to the user. So, let's add more validations to our script. We, as the creators of the script, know that the script is failing because the second argument should be a number – an integer, to be more precise. However, this validation can be slightly tricky because of the way a lot of programming languages behave, including Ruby and PHP. The behavior I'm referring to is the way Ruby converts a text string into an integer. As an example, a string such as `'22'` will be converted into an integer, `22`. However, the `'henry'` string will unexpectedly be converted into a valid `0`, and while this is not what we need, we can certainly take advantage of this behavior. For our script, we need the second argument to be larger than `0`. So, that's exactly what we are going to validate:

```ruby
# validate_arguments.rb

if ARGV.size != 2
  puts "Error. The script has failed!"
  puts "Usage: ruby validate_arguments.rb name times_to_repeat"
  Kernel::exit(1)
end

input_arguments = ARGV
name = input_arguments.first
cycle_times = input_arguments.last.to_i

if cycle_times < 1
  puts "Error. The second argument has to be an integer!"
  puts "Usage: ruby validate_arguments.rb name times_to_repeat"
  Kernel::exit(1)
end

cycle_times.times { puts name }
puts "But we are still running the script"
```

Let's run the script with the incorrect arguments again:

```
ruby validate_arguments.rb 3 henry
```

We will get the following output:

```
Error. The second argument has to be an integer!
Usage: ruby validate_arguments.rb name times_to_repeat
```

With that, we have successfully made our script validate that the input must be two arguments. If we feed the script either no arguments, one argument, or more than two arguments, it will fail and send an error message describing the correct usage of the script. Now that we've looked into different ways to add input to our script, let's look at another way to interact with the user: user input.

User input

So far, we've made use of command-line arguments to make our scripts more generic, thus helping with what could be an automated script. Be it a shell script (as we've done so far) or a crontab script to be run at a designated time each day, we've learned the basic usage of these arguments that are fed to our scripts. But there is another type of argument that, while technically not a command-line argument, is closely related and is super useful when making scripts that interact with human users. In comes *user input*. User input helps us make a script more interactive with the user as it makes a pause in the execution of the script to wait for the user to type data and resume after the user has typed a carriage return (or the *Enter* key). This makes a more user-friendly interaction with the user. Let's look at a simple example to see this interaction at play. We will create a file called user_input. rb and add the following code:

```
# user_input.rb
puts "Enter your name:"
name = gets
puts "Hello #{name}"
```

Now, let's run it on our shell:

```
ruby user_input.rb
```

We will notice that the output shows the following message:

```
Enter your name:
```

We will also notice that the shell looks slightly different as it is expecting input from us. So, let's do that and type a name, hitting the *Enter* key right after entering it:

```
Enter your name:
brandon
```

Immediately, the execution of our script continues and outputs the greeting that we included in our code:

```
Enter your name:
brandon
Hello brandon
```

Notice how interactive our script has become. It asks for your name; we type the name and immediately we are greeted. While this is friendlier and more interactive, we still need to fix a couple of things in our code. The method we are currently using (`Kernel::gets()`; see `https://ruby-doc.org/2.7.7/Kernel.html#method-i-gets`) not only includes the name, but it also includes the return of carriage character (\n) or in layman's terms, the *Enter* key character. So, if we tried to compare the input to a string, we would be surprised to see that it wouldn't behave as we would expect it to. Let's try it with the following code:

```
# user_input.rb
puts "Enter your name:"
name = gets
puts "Hello #{name}" if name == "brandon"
```

Now, let's re-run our script:

```
ruby user_input.rb
```

Let's input the name `brandon`:

```
Enter your name:
brandon
```

This time, notice that we don't see the greeting. And this is not because of a typo. This is because the `Kernel::gets()` method is capturing a character at the end of the name. In comes another method to save the day: `chomp()`. The `chomp()` method removes carriage return characters and trailing new lines from the string. Please refer to `https://apidock.com/ruby/String/chomp` for more details regarding this method. Essentially, it cleans up our string and leaves the original text. So, let's modify our code so that it includes this method. Our code will now look like this:

```
# user_input.rb
puts "Enter your name:"
name = gets.chomp
puts "Hello #{name}" if name == "brandon"
```

Let's run it once more:

```
ruby user_input.rb
```

If we input the name `brandon` again, we will get the following result:

```
Enter your name:
brandon
Hello brandon
```

We will finally get the correct greeting. So, from now on, we will get input from the user with `gets.chomp` for safe measure. Now, let's fetch an integer from the user and run some code multiple times, depending on the number the user typed:

```ruby
# user_input.rb
puts "Enter your name:"
name = gets.chomp
puts "Hello #{name}" if name == "brandon"
puts "Enter the number of times to try the process"
repeat_n = gets.chomp.to_i
repeat_n.times do
  puts "trying..."
  sleep(1)
end
```

Let's run it on the shell again:

ruby user_input.rb

Now, let's input the name `brandon` and enter 3 afterwards. This will be the whole sequence:

```
Enter your name:
brandon
Hello brandon
Enter times you would like to try the process:
3
trying...
trying...
trying...
```

After entering `brandon`, we now output instructions to enter a digit, and right after that, we fetch an integer from the user. With this digit, we will print a `trying...` message and use the `sleep()` method to pause the execution for 1 second. If you would like more detailed information regarding the `sleep()` method, please check out `https://apidock.com/ruby/Kernel/sleep`. You will notice that the script will show the `trying...` message, pause for a second, show the second message, pause again, and finally show the last message, pause one last time, and finish the execution of the script. The `sleep()` method is useful when we are waiting for a process to finish. It's especially useful when working with API calls, which may take some time to finish. As a final exercise, let's dive into a script's friendliness and usefulness.

Putting it all together

Reading and understanding someone else's code is essential to learning Ruby. With that intent, we will now look at the following example, which was written with some of the techniques we learned about in this chapter, and figure out what the script is doing:

```ruby
# main.rb
# Section 1: Ruby version validation
if Gem::Version.new(RUBY_VERSION) < Gem::Version.new('2.6')
  puts "Please verify the Ruby version!"
  Kernel::exit(1)
end


# Section 2: Open or create user_name file
file_instance = File.open("user_name.txt", "a+")
user_name = file_instance.read

# Section 3: Empty name validation
if user_name.empty?
  puts "Enter your name:"
  name = gets.chomp
  File.write("user_name.txt", name)
  # Section 4: Program main log
  File.write("main.log", "Writing #{name} as the entry to user_name.
txt at #{Time.now}\n", mode: "a")
  user_name =  name
end


# Section 5: Program title
puts "Hello #{user_name.capitalize}"
puts "Welcome to Chapter 4"
puts "Please enter how many times you would like to make a log entry"

# Section 6: Program cycle
repeat_n = gets.chomp.to_i

repeat_n.times do
  puts "Adding log entry..."
  File.write("main.log", "Adding entry to log at #{Time.now}\n", mode:
"a")
  sleep(1)
end
```

For us to understand the intent of the script, we will divide it into six sections that we have commented on the code itself. This is not compulsory when writing code, but I've taken the liberty to do this for teaching purposes. So, let's take a look at the first section:

```
...
# Section 1: Ruby version validation
if Gem::Version.new(RUBY_VERSION) < Gem::Version.new('2.6')
  puts "Please verify the Ruby version!"
  Kernel::exit(1)
end
...
```

Here, we are comparing our currently installed Ruby version and making sure that the version is higher than 2.6. If the version is lower than that, we print an error message and exit the program. This is something you might find very often in scripts as major versions tend to differ in terms of functionality and sometimes in syntax.

Let's move on to the next section of our script:

```
...
# Section 2: Open or create user_name file
file_instance = File.open("user_name.txt", "a+")
user_name = file_instance.read
...
```

In this section, we are opening a file, but as we've seen in previous examples, it's using "a+" mode so that if the file does not exist, it creates it. If the file already exists, it reads its contents. The script's intent in this section is to read a user's name from this file, but if the file is empty, the name will be empty too. This may seem slightly different from what we've been doing so far. However, let's look at the next section, where this will make more sense. In sections 3 and 4, we can see the following:

```
...
# Section 3: Empty name validation
if user_name.empty?
  puts "Enter your name:"
  name = gets.chomp
  File.write("user_name.txt", name)
  # Section 4: Program main log
  File.write("main.log", "Writing #{name} as the entry to user_name.
txt at #{Time.now}\n", mode: "a")
  user_name =  name
end
...
```

In section 3, we can see that if the username fetched from the file is not empty, the script moves on to the next section. But if the username is empty, then we prompt the user to provide a username. Once the user types a username, the script will write the name to the `user_name.txt` file and move to section 4.

In section 4, the script simply writes a log entry to a `main.log` file in which it writes the name obtained from the user and the time in which the user did this. Lastly, the script assigns the `user_name` variable to be used later on in the script.

In section 5, we have this code:

```
...
# Section 5: Program title
puts "Hello #{user_name.capitalize}"
puts "Welcome to Chapter 4"
puts "Please enter how many times you would like to make a log entry"
...
```

In this section, we greet the user by capitalizing the name, print a welcoming message, and then print another aiding message so that the user knows what they'll do next, which is enter a number.

In our last section, we are doing something similar to what we did in our previous looping example. Let's take a look:

```
...
# Section 6: Program cycle
repeat_n = gets.chomp.to_i

repeat_n.times do
  puts "Adding log entry..."
  File.write("main.log", "Adding entry to log at #{Time.now}\n", mode:
"a")
  sleep(1)
end
...
```

In section 6, which is the last section of the script, we're getting a number from the user, then taking this number and doing a cycle to execute a code the number of times the user provided. The code to be executed simply shows a message for the user and adds multiple entry logs to the same `main.log` file. In this case, the script is also using the append writing mode so that when the script writes to this file, it will write contents at the end of the file instead of replacing the previous contents. This type of logging is both common and useful in the scripting and programming realms. It helps other users debug the functionality of the script, especially when things start failing. We are only missing one thing now: running the script. Let's run it:

```
ruby main.rb
```

The first time we run this file, we will get the following output on the shell:

```
Enter your name:
```

Let's enter `daniel`. After we enter this name, we will get the following output:

```
Hello Daniel
Welcome to chapter 4
Please enter how many times you would like to make a log entry
```

Here, the script requires that we enter a number. Let's type 2. The script will respond with the following output:

```
Adding log entry...
Adding log entry...
```

Initially, this seems simple enough. However, if we take a look at the contents of the folder where our script resides, we'll notice two new files: `main.log` and `user_name.txt` . If we open the `user_name.txt` file, its contents will coincide with the name we typed:

```
daniel
```

And if we look at the `main.log` file, we will see the following output:

```
Writing daniel as the entry to user_name.txt at 2022-12-25 16:33:24
-0600
Adding entry to log at 2022-12-25 16:34:53 -0600
Adding entry to log at 2022-12-25 16:34:54 -0600
```

This content coincides with what happened on the initial run of the script. It wrote `daniel` to the log and added two entries to the same log. Now, let's run the script once more:

```
ruby main.rb
```

This time, we will notice that the script does not ask for a user, instead using the previous username we entered. The output will look like this:

```
Hello Daniel
Welcome to Chapter 4
Please enter how many times you would like to make a log entry
```

This is very practical as we don't need to enter the name every time we run the script. Lastly, it prompts us for a number to run the log process again. Let's type 1 and wait for the response, which should look like this:

```
Adding log entry...
```

This time, as we typed 1, the cycle only ran the code once, which is what we expected. I hope you found this reading exercise useful and I hope you make the habit of reading other developer's code to both learn good practices and understand how to do things in Ruby.

Summary

In this chapter, we learned how to write more useful scripts that we will probably reuse in the future. We also got a glimpse at some of the tools that Ruby has to handle text. We also learned how to open, read, and write content to and from a file and how this may come in handy when writing scripts. Lastly, we were exposed to Ruby's command-line arguments, which make our automation work easier. We also learned of Ruby's user input arguments, which make our scripts more interactive for users. Having learned this, we are now ready to undercover some misconceptions about PHP, Ruby, Ruby on Rails, and other frameworks.

5
Libraries and Class Syntax

So far, we've only worked with Ruby and its core components without the advantage of other libraries that are available in Ruby. Additionally, we've only taken a partial peek at Ruby objects and classes. In this chapter, we will take a test drive with you to learn about Ruby libraries (gems) and how we can take advantage of the Gemfile to do so. Lastly, we'll also learn the basics of class syntax to help us move toward more advanced tools, such as Ruby on Rails.

With that in mind, in this chapter, we will cover the following topics:

- Let's get ready to bundle!!!
- Gemfile versus `composer.json`
- Integrating libraries into your code in Ruby
- Declaring classes in Ruby
- Objects in Ruby
- Inheritance in Ruby

Technical requirements

To follow along this chapter, we will need the following:

- Any IDE to view/edit code (e.g., SublimeText, Visual Studio Code, Notepad++, Vim, Emacs, etc.)
- For macOS users, you will also need to have Xcode Command Line Tools installed
- Ruby version 2.6 or later installed and ready to use

The code presented in this chapter is available at `https://github.com/PacktPublishing/From-PHP-to-Ruby-on-Rails/`.

Let's get ready to bundle!!!

Programming languages by themselves, while useful, can't take into account every single use case that a programmer might encounter. The core of the language includes many useful libraries, so out of the box, the language is quite useful. This is true for most programming languages. However, there comes a time when we need to go beyond the core library and use other libraries to solve our issues at hand. In Ruby, the community has created a number of libraries, fondly named *gems*. To keep track of these gems, the Ruby community has come up with a tool called *bundler*. To season PHP developers, the PHP counterpart for the bundler is Composer (`https://getcomposer.org/`). The two work for the same purpose (managing libraries), but bundler works slightly differently in that it installs the libraries in the computer, while Composer merely makes them available for your project. But wait – we haven't even installed a library yet. Let's take a step back and install a Ruby gem.

Installing a gem

Before letting bundler take over, we should understand what and how to install gems on our system. Ruby has the ability to parse JSON objects, but there is a gem called `oj` that is more efficient in handling JSON strings and converting them to Ruby hashes. Let's first install the `oj` gem. In a shell, let's type the following commands:

```
gem install oj
```

We should get the following output after running the preceding command and pressing the *Enter* key:

```
Fetching oj-3.14.2.gem
Building native extensions. This could take a while...
Successfully installed oj-3.14.2
Parsing documentation for oj-3.14.2
Installing ri documentation for oj-3.14.2
Done installing documentation for oj after 2 seconds
1 gem installed
```

Congratulations! We have installed our first gem and are now ready to use it within our code. Let's put this gem to the test by creating a file called `reading_json.rb` and adding the following code:

```
json_text = '{"name":"Sarah Kerrigan", "age":23, "human":
  true}'
ruby_hash = Oj.load(json_text)
puts ruby_hash
puts ruby_hash["name"]
```

Now, let's go back to our shell and try to execute the following script:

```
ruby reading_json.rb
```

We will get the following error:

```
reading_json.rb:5:in `<main>': uninitialized constant Oj (NameError)
```

Why is our script failing? Well, we installed our gem and did not get any errors while doing so. As it turns out, we not only need to install our gem but also need to import it within our code. Let's do that at the beginning of our file, so our code will now look like this:

```
require 'oj'
json_text = '{"name":"Sarah Kerrigan", "age":23, "human":
  true}'
ruby_hash = Oj.load(json_text)
puts ruby_hash
puts ruby_hash["name"]
```

Then, let's execute our script again with the following:

```
ruby reading_json.rb
```

Now, we will get the correct output:

```
{"name"=>"Sarah Kerrigan", "age"=>23, "human"=>true}
Sarah Kerrigan
```

As you can see, we've converted a JSON string into a Ruby hash, and it is now ready to be used within our script. This is useful when loading configuration from a JSON file or when processing an API call that returns a JSON response. However, there is one issue that we have not dealt with yet. How can we make sure that other people who use our script will have the same results? Well, this is the cue for both bundler and the Gemfile to enter our scene.

Gemfile versus composer.json

As I mentioned before, bundler helps us handle all our program's dependencies – that is, everything we need to install in order for our program to run correctly. To accomplish this, bundler uses a text file, which we will call a `Gemfile`. Composer works in a very similar way by having us create a file called `composer.json`, but while Composer downloads the required libraries into a folder, bundler installs them on our system. If bundler determines that a dependency is missing, it will automatically try to install it. Ruby's way is a bit more magical (or automatic). Let's take bundler for a test drive to understand the process a little further. We will start by uninstalling our previously installed `oj` gem with the following command in the shell:

```
gem uninstall oj
```

The preceding command will confirm when the gem is removed from our system:

```
Successfully uninstalled oj-3.14.2
```

Now, if we try to run our `reading_json.rb` again, we will get the following error:

```
...kernel_require.rb:54:in `require': cannot load such file -- oj
(LoadError)
    from...kernel_require.rb:54:in `require'
    from reading_json.rb:1:in `<main>'
```

We are back to where we started, but now we will solve our library (or gem) installation with a Gemfile. Let's create a file called `Gemfile` with the following content:

```
source 'https://rubygems.org'
gem 'oj'
```

With this, we tell bundler where to download the dependencies and what our dependencies are. We could tell bundler other things, such as the gem version or even what Ruby version (or equivalent) to use, but for now, we'll keep it simple. Now, let's try it. On a shell, let's type the following command:

```
bundle install
```

Depending on the operating system that you're using, you may need to type your root or administrator password, but once you do, the output of the command should be as follows:

```
Fetching gem metadata from https://rubygems.org/..
Resolving dependencies...
Using bundler 1.17.2

Installing oj 3.14.2 with native extensions
Bundle complete! 1 Gemfile dependency, 2 gems now installed.
Use `bundle info [gemname]` to see where a bundled gem is installed.
```

Now that our gem is installed, we can safely run our script again with the following command:

```
ruby reading_json.rb
```

We should get the exact same output as before:

```
{"name"=>"Sarah Kerrigan", "age"=>23, "human"=>true}
Sarah Kerrigan
```

However, now we will notice something slightly different. If we look at the contents of the folder where we have our script and the Gemfile, we also have a new file called `Gemfile.lock`. Also, if we look at the contents, there should be something similar to this:

```
GEM
  remote: https://rubygems.org/
  specs:
    oj (3.14.2)
```

```
PLATFORMS
   ruby
DEPENDENCIES
   oj
BUNDLED WITH
    1.17.2
```

The `Gemfile.lock` file serves as a map of dependencies. If there is no map, bundler has to build it from scratch, and this process sometimes takes a while. However, if there is a lock file, even if the dependencies have not been installed, the process of installing them is much more efficient.

We've come a long way from just installing a gem to now creating the ideal scenario for our script to run. In the next section, we'll look at additional options (such as using a specific version of a gem) that we can set with our Gemfile to add further specificity to our Ruby environment.

Integrating libraries into your code in Ruby

One of the most useful skills you should acquire in your path to becoming a seasoned Ruby developer is integrating other gems into your code. As we've seen before, this is accomplished by using the Gemfile, but we'll look at some additional options we can add to it and integrate them into our own scripts. Let's write a script that takes the GitHub public API and lists all of the public repos for the user `@PacktPublishing`. There are several ways we could do this, but for this example, I've chosen a gem called **Faraday**. You can take a look at the source code here: `https://github.com/lostisland/faraday`.

Faraday is a client library that can help us make **Representational State Transfer** (**REST**) calls that are much easier to read than using the native `Net::HTTP` library that comes with Ruby. Let's create a folder called `integrating_gems` and navigate to that folder:

```
mkdir integrating_gems
cd integrating_gems
```

Now, let's create a file called `Gemfile` with the following content:

```
source 'https://rubygems.org'
gem 'oj'
gem 'faraday'
```

Before installing these gems, I'd like to use more options available in the Gemfile syntax. We're going to lock the Faraday version at 2.5, which simply means that we install a specific version. So, let's change the Faraday line to the following:

```
gem 'faraday', '2.5'
```

Locking to a version has, of course, its advantages and its disadvantages. Among the advantages is that you can be sure that the script will work the same way, with usually the same syntax, in several environments. The downside is that you probably would be locked to a Ruby version, and you could end up in a scenario where you won't be able to upgrade Ruby until you upgrade the gem. For the `oj` gem, we will use the ~ operator and set it to the following:

```
gem 'oj', '~> 3.13.0'
```

The ~ operator is used to delimit ranges of versions. In this specific case, we tell bundler to get the highest released version between 3.13.0 and 3.14, excluding 3.14 – in other words, we require a version larger or equal to 3.13 but less than 3.14. So, why use this operator? Well, in short, the ~ operator is used to increase stability within our dependencies. I won't go into depth as to why we would use this syntax. Just know that you will encounter it sooner or later.

Should you want to dig deeper into this topic, please refer to the following links:

- `https://thoughtbot.com/blog/rubys-pessimistic-operator`
- `https://guides.rubygems.org/patterns/#declaring_dependencies`

Our Gemfile will now look like this:

```
source 'https://rubygems.org'
gem 'oj', '~> 3.13.0'
gem 'faraday', '2.5'
```

Now, let's install our dependencies again with bundler. On a shell, type in the following command:

```
bundle install
```

We'll get output similar to this:

```
Fetching gem metadata from https://rubygems.org/........
Resolving dependencies...
Using bundler 1.17.2
Using faraday-net_http 2.1.0
Following files may not be writable, so sudo is needed:
  /usr/local/bin
Using ruby2_keywords 0.0.5
Using faraday 2.5.0
Using oj 3.13.23
Bundle complete! 2 Gemfile dependencies, 5 gems now installed.
Use `bundle info [gemname]` to see where a bundled gem is installed.
```

Now, with our gems ready, we can use them in our script. Let's create a script called `faraday_example.rb` with the following content:

```
require 'faraday'
require 'oj'
conn = Faraday.new(
  url: 'https://api.github.com',
  headers: {'Content-Type' '> 'application/json'}
)
```

Let's take a step back and see what we are doing. We're importing the `faraday` and `oj` gems. Then, we're creating a client that will connect to the GitHub API. The client object requires a URL and some headers, which we provided. So far, we have not called the API yet. Let's do that. At the end of the file, add the call to the API and output the response with the following:

```
response = conn.get('/users/PacktPublishing/repos')
puts response.body
```

Now, let's try to execute this script with the following:

```
ruby faraday_example.rb
```

This will output a lot of text, so I'm going to include only an excerpt:

```
[{"id":184740404,"node_
id":"MDEwOlJlcG9zaXRvcnkxODQ3NDA0MDQ=","name":"-.NET-Core-
Microservices","full_name":"PacktPublishing/-.NET-Core-Microservices
","private":false,"owner":{"login":"PacktPublishing","id":10974906,"n
ode_id":"MDEyOk9yZ2FuaXphdGlvbjEwOTc0OTA2"
  ...
```

With that output, we can confirm that we have successfully connected to the GitHub API. For the last part of the exercise, let's use the `oj` gem to convert the JSON text to a Ruby hash and output the names of all of the responses that the API returned. So, let's remove the `puts` command and replace it with an `oj` object. Our code will look like this now:

```
require 'faraday'
require 'oj'
conn = Faraday.new(
  url: 'https://api.github.com',
  headers: {'Content-Type' => 'application/json'}
)
response = conn.get('/users/PacktPublishing/repos')
repo_hash = Oj.load(response.body)
```

So, we've taken the response from the GitHub API service and converted it to a Ruby hash. Lastly, let's output the names of the repos by adding the following to the end of the script:

```
repo_hash.each { |repo| puts repo['name'] }
```

If we run the script one last time, an excerpt from the output will look like this:

```
-.NET-Core-Microservices
-Accelerate-Deep-Learning-on-Raspberry-Pi
-Accelerate-Deep-Learning-on-Raspberry-Pi-
…
```

With that, we've successfully connected to an API with the Faraday gem and processed the output with the `oj` gem. For reference, this is what the code should ultimately look like:

```
require 'faraday'
require 'oj'
conn = Faraday.new(
  url: 'https://api.github.com',
  headers: {'Content-Type' => 'application/json'}
)
response = conn.get('/users/PacktPublishing/repos')
repo_hash = Oj.load(response.body)
repo_hash.each { |repo| puts repo['name'] }
```

This is the starting point for how to share code to be run in other environments. Should we want others to be able to run our script, we should include both the script and the Gemfile with our shared code so that others know what needs to be installed before running the scripts.

Also, just so you know, this was merely an exercise to learn how to include and use gems within our code. The syntax on the Gemfile was only procured for learning purposes. You should always aspire to have the latest version of a gem. However, locking to a version is useful when you want to have control of when and where you do upgrades.

Now that we've established how gems work and their usage, we can now move on to object-oriented programming in Ruby.

Declaring classes in Ruby

Both PHP and Ruby are languages that use the **Object-Oriented Programming** (**OOP**) paradigm, Ruby by design and PHP by its own evolution. By now, serious developers should be very familiar with the paradigm. In PHP, all frameworks use OOP. While we are not going to go in depth into how this paradigm is implemented in Ruby, we will go through the basics of class syntax.

A class is basically an abstraction of a real-world entity. It is the blueprint of this abstraction. Let's start by creating a simple class representing a person, some attributes for this person, and an action (or method) for them. Let's create a file called `class_syntax.rb` with the following content:

```
class Person
end
```

This is as simple as it gets, but this by itself is not very useful. For this to be useful, we need to add attributes that represent the characteristics of a person. So, let's add some attributes such as their first name and their last name. Our code will now look like this:

```
class Person
  @first_name = nil
  @last_name = nil
end
```

Note that we have defined our attributes by prepending them with @. These are called instance variables and can only be accessed by a method. Now, let's define a method to print out the full name:

```
class Person
  @first_name = nil
  @last_name = nil
  def full_name
    puts "#{@first_name} #{@last_name}"
  end
end
```

With the exception of the instance variable, note that we are not doing anything we have not learned before. We defined a method (or function), and we included the first and last name variables on the string to be printed by the method. One last thing we will do to this blueprint is add a constructor. In OOP, a constructor is a method that can be customized to add behaviors and attributes when we create an object with a class definition. In other words, when we take the blueprint, we define and use it to create a specific object, and we can control certain values at the time of creation of the object. In PHP, this method is implemented by simply naming the method `__constructor()`. Its equivalent in Ruby is naming the method `initialize()`. Let's now include it in our class definition. Our class definition should look like this:

```
class Person
  def initialize
    @first_name = 'James'
    @last_name = 'Raynor'
  end
  def full_name
    puts "#{@first_name} #{@last_name}"
```

```
      end
  end
```

Note that we no longer need the instance variable definition, as this is done on the constructor (initializer). Congratulations! Our first class is ready to be used. Let's now move on to the next section to create our first object using this class definition.

Objects in Ruby

In the previous section, we defined what our abstraction of a person should look like. It is a person that will have a first name and a last name, and we will be able to print out their full name. In parallel to the construction business, since we now have a blueprint, we are now ready to erect our building with these specifications. This creation is what we call an instance or an object of a class. The class definition is generic and the instance is specific. Without going too deep into this relationship between a class definition and an object, we'll take a look at what this relationship looks like in code and how this will help us make better and more readable code. Let's take our previous code and create our first object:

```
# class_syntax.rb
class Person
  def initialize
   @first_name = 'James'
   @last_name = 'Raynor'
  end
  def full_name
    puts "#{@first_name} #{@last_name}"
  end
end
person = Person.new
```

We've now created a specific person based on our class, and we are now ready to call some of the methods for that person. We can now call the `full_name()` method. Let's do that by adding the following line to the end of our file:

```
person.full_name
```

Let's run our script again from the shell with the following:

```
ruby class_syntax.rb
```

Then, we should get the following output:

```
James Raynor
```

And voilà! We've finally given our class a more practical use. We are now able to create as many objects (persons) as we want with the class definition. However, we still have an issue. Our class only lets us create persons that are named James Raynor. We wanted specificity, but this turned out to be too specific. We need to modify our class so that we can create more generic objects. So, let's do that by adding parameters to our constructor. Our code will now look like the following:

```ruby
# class_syntax.rb
class Person
  def initialize( first_name, last_name )
   @first_name = first_name
   @last_name = last_name
  end
  def full_name
    puts "#{@first_name} #{@last_name}"
  end
end
person = Person.new
person.full_name
```

We've added two parameters to our constructor method. The first name we pass to our class will be assigned to our instance variable, @first_name, so that it will be available to other methods. The same goes for the last name. An additional adjustment that we must make now is to pass the first and last names to our constructor. So, let's do that:

```ruby
# class_syntax.rb
class Person
  def initialize( first_name, last_name )
   @first_name = first_name
   @last_name = last_name
  end
  def full_name
    puts "#{@first_name} #{@last_name}"
  end
end
jim = Person.new( 'James', 'Raynor' )
jim.full_name
```

Now, we can create as many instances (or objects) as we want. Let's add two more people:

```ruby
# class_syntax.rb
class Person
  def initialize( first_name, last_name )
   @first_name = first_name
   @last_name = last_name
```

```
  end
  def full_name
    puts "#{@first_name} #{@last_name}"
  end
end
jim = Person.new( 'James', 'Raynor' )
sarah = Person.new( 'Sarah', 'Kerrigan' )
arcturus = Person.new( 'Arcturus', 'Mengsk' )
jim.full_name
sarah.full_name
arcturus.full_name
```

Now, let's run our script on our shell:

```
ruby class_syntax.rb
```

The output will be the following:

```
James Raynor
Sarah Kerrigan
Arcturus Mengsk
```

We've made our blueprint more generic, and we can now create different characters from that blueprint.

Before moving on to our next topic inheritance, I want us to take a look at a class tool that you will encounter in the future and that you'll find extremely useful – attribute accessors.

Attribute accessors

In our class definition, we have the `first_name` and `last_name` attributes, and we also have a `full_name()` method. However, what if we wanted to output the person's first name? We might be tempted to try the following:

```
jim.first_name
```

However, this would fail miserably with the following error:

```
class_syntax.rb:23:in `<main>': undefined method `first_name' for
#<Person:0x000000014d935460> (NoMethodError)
```

This is where Ruby deviates from how PHP would look or behave. Ruby can apparently have a method and an attribute with the same name. While this is not technically true, let's for argument's sake say that it is so that we can momentarily move forward with the exercise. Let's create a method called first_name:

```
...
def first_name
  @first_name
end
...
```

The method looks strange, but let's remember that Ruby doesn't need us to explicitly return a value as it does it automatically. So, the method is simply returning the value contained in @first_name. While useful, we would have to do this for every attribute we defined. Additionally, we only created the method to obtain the value. We would also need to create a method to set the value. However, I have some good news for you. Ruby has already solved this issue with attribute accessors. An attribute accessor automatically creates the methods to get and set the value. We only need to indicate which attribute we want this "magic" to have. Let's define the attribute accessors and then exploit them. Our final code should look like this:

```
# class_syntax.rb
class Person
  attr_accessor :first_name, :last_name
  def initialize( first_name, last_name )
   @first_name = first_name
   @last_name = last_name
  end
  def full_name
    puts "#{first_name} #{last_name}"
  end
end
jim = Person.new( 'James', 'Raynor' )
sarah = Person.new( 'Sarah', 'Kerrigan' )
arcturus = Person.new( 'Arcturus', 'Mengsk' )
jim.full_name
sarah.full_name
arcturus.full_name
puts jim.first_name
puts sarah.first_name
puts arcturus.last_name
```

Let's run it again with the following command:

```
ruby class_syntax.rb
```

We should get the following output:

```
James Raynor
Sarah Kerrigan
Arcturus Mengsk
James
Sarah
Mengsk
```

Note how we did not have to define the `last_name` method, and yet it's available. At some point in your path towards learning Ruby, I guarantee you will encounter the `attr_accessor` tool. Ruby also has `attr_reader` and `attr_writer`, which separate into two methods what `attr_accessor` does by itself. Should you want to go more in depth into attribute accessors, what they do exactly, and see other examples, you may want to visit `https://www.rubyguides.com/2018/11/attr_accessor/`.

Are you ready to make more powerful classes? Then, let's hop to the next section.

Inheritance in Ruby

So far, we've looked at a few features that come with Ruby's implementation of the OOP paradigm, but we have neglected to look at one of the core features that help us recycle code. Inheritance can be simplified as the practice of passing the features of a class to create a brand-new child class. With this new class, we can use any of the features from the parent class, create new features, or customize the features that come from the parent class. The syntax for inheritance can be quite different than in PHP, but the behavior is quite similar. With that in mind, let's take a look at a few use cases and see it in action.

Let's say we wanted a class that would let us connect to a database. Instead of having to write all the functionality to connect to a database, we could get an already created database class, create a new one that inherited all the database functionality, and then focus on creating just the features that we need. This is one way to reuse code with inheritance, but let's use a simpler example so that we can see inheritance in practice. Let's say we wanted to make an abstraction of a user. The user must have first name, last name, age, and email details. We can take the `Person` class, defined in the previous section, inherit the features in our new `User` class, and just focus on the missing pieces.

So, let's take our `Person` class and create a file called `inheritance_example.rb` with the following content:

```ruby
# inheritance_example.rb
class Person
  attr_accessor :first_name, :last_name
  def initialize( first_name, last_name )
   @first_name = first_name
```

```
    @last_name = last_name
  end
  def full_name
    puts "#{first_name} #{last_name}"
  end
end
```

Now, let's create a new class below our original class called `User` and inherit from the `Person` class. We'll do this with the < operator. Let's add this to the end of our `Person` class:

```
# inheritance_example.rb
...
class User < Person
end
```

With just two lines of code, we've made a brand-new class that behaves (for now) in the exact same way as the `Person` class. Let's confirm that by creating a new `User` object. Let's now add the following to the end of our file:

```
# inheritance_example.rb
...
user = User.new
```

Now, let's try to run this script from our shell:

ruby inheritance_example.rb

This should output the following:

```
inheritance_example.rb:4:in `initialize': wrong number of arguments
(given 0, expected 2) (ArgumentError)
  from inheritance_example.rb:18:in `new'
  from inheritance_example.rb:18:in `<main>'
```

Our script failed, but why? As we read through the message, it states that the constructor expected two parameters, but none were given. From our previous execution example, we can infer that we have to give our constructor the parameters for the first name and last name. So, let's add those parameters, and let's also call the `full_name()` method. Our code will now look like this:

```
class Person
  attr_accessor :first_name, :last_name
  def initialize( first_name, last_name )
   @first_name = first_name
   @last_name = last_name
  end
  def full_name
```

```
    puts "#{first_name} #{last_name}"
  end
end
class User < Person
end
user = User.new
user = User.new("Amit", "Seth")
user.full_name
```

Let's run this script:

ruby inheritance_example.rb

The script will output the following:

Amit Seth

So, we have confirmed that, out of the box, this newly created class has inherited all of its functionality from the Person class. Nowhere did we have to define the full_name() method, as it's already available. Additionally, the constructor automatically assigned the first and last name to our @first_name and @last_name instance variables, respectively. Again, we only had to have this class inherit from the Person class. However, using the example that we provided at the beginning of this section, we want to add an additional attribute called email. So first, we will add an attribute accessor for the email attribute. Our User class now looks like this:

```
class User < Person
  attr_accessor :email
end
```

We can now assign the em.ail attribute from our object with the following:

```
user.email = "my@fakemail.com"
```

However, what we want to do is include this assignment in the new User constructor. This is not as easy as it seems, but it's not that difficult either. So, we first have to define a constructor for our new User class. Let's do just that. Our User class will look like this now:

```
class User < Person
  attr_accessor :email
  def initialize( email )
    @email = email
  end
end
```

However, by doing this, we've overwritten the original constructor method (initializer). But do not despair, as the original constructor is still available via the super() method. The super() method calls the original constructor, but you must provide the original number of arguments. So, to finish this example, let's again add the first name, last name, and email to our constructor and, finally, call the super() method. Our final code will look like this:

```ruby
class Person
  attr_accessor :first_name, :last_name
  def initialize( first_name, last_name )
   @first_name = first_name
   @last_name = last_name
  end
  def full_name
    puts "#{first_name} #{last_name}"
  end
end
class User < Person
  attr_accessor :email
  def initialize( first_name, last_name, email )
    @email = email
    super( first_name, last_name )
  end
end
user = User.new
user = User.new("Amit", "Seth")
user.full_name
puts user.email
```

We've successfully used inheritance to reuse our Person class functionality and built a new class called User. When talking about classes using inheritance, you'll hear the term hierarchy. When talking about hierarchy, we're referring to the position on an imaginary structure of our classes where on the top, we will have the most generic class and on the bottom the most specific class. For this example, the hierarchical relationship between the Person class and the User class may start to make sense, with the Person class being the most generic class and thus the one on top. In other words, a user is a person; thus, the person must have the attributes of a user and a person. The opposite is not true. A person may no necessarily be a user. A person could be a client and have a different use case where we don't need the email attribute. While designing your Ruby classes, if you take into account this hierarchy, it will be easier for you to determine what functionality should go where to write less code and not have issues with repeating unnecessary code. While this example is extremely simplified, it showed us how easy it is to build reusable classes.

Summary

In this chapter, we learned how Ruby libraries are installed, used, and named (gems). We also learned to use the bundler tool to install gems, creating environments for our scripts and programs to function correctly. Lastly, we learned the most basic OOP syntax to both create, instantiate, and inherit classes. Now, we are ready to start debugging.

Debugging Ruby

Just like with any other significant programming language, Ruby has a number of tools to help us analyze, fix, and improve our code. According to a software architect I encountered many years ago, the disparity between a programmer who possesses debugging skills and one who lacks them equates to the distinction between a junior programmer and a senior programmer. By using the right tools to debug our code, we can both improve our code and improve our understanding of how the language is interpreted, which in the long run, is beneficial to our path as developers. Let's take a look at the tools that come with Ruby out of the box, as well as the gems that the Ruby community has developed to debug our code.

With debugging in mind, in this chapter, we will cover the following topics:

- Debugging functions in Ruby versus PHP

- Gems for debugging

- Understanding **Interactive Ruby** (IRB)'s usefulness

Technical requirements

To follow along with this chapter, you will need the following:

- Any IDE to view/edit code (e.g., Sublime Text, Visual Studio Code, Notepad++, Vim, Emacs, etc.)

- For macOS users, you will also need to have Xcode Command Line Tools installed

- Ruby version 2.6 or later installed and ready to use

The code presented in this chapter is available at `https://github.com/PacktPublishing/From-PHP-to-Ruby-on-Rails/`.

Debugging functions in Ruby versus PHP

So far, we've made scripts and code snippets making sure that our code works correctly every time. However, in the real world, we'll come into contact with code that someone else has created and either wasn't tested, or it wasn't tested in a scenario that hadn't come up until now. This happens more often than not, and we should be prepared to get our hands dirty to fix these types of issues. In PHP, we have a couple of functions that will help us debug in the simplest way. You are welcome to just read the following example and not follow along. For now, let's take a look at PHP's `var_dump()` function. We can open a command shell and create a file with the following content:

```php
<?php //buggy_code.php
$person['firSt'] = 'Thomas';
$person['last'] = 'Anderson';
echo "Hi {$person['first']} {$person['last']}";
```

Let's say we ran the following PHP script on our shell:

```
php buggy_code.php
```

It should output something similar to this:

```
PHP Warning:  Undefined array key "first"…
Warning: Undefined array key "first" in…
Hi  Anderson
```

At first glance, we may or may not see the error within the code. If you saw the error at first glance, congratulations, you're off to a good start. But for those who didn't see the error at first glance, let's use the `var_dump()` function. Let's comment out the last line and add this to the ending line of our code:

```php
<?php //buggy_code.php
…
//echo "Hi {$person['first']} {$person['last']}";
var_dump($person);
```

And let's run this script again from our shell:

```
php buggy_code.php
```

This should output the following:

```
…
array(2) {
  ["firSt"]=>
  string(6) "Thomas"
  ["last"]=>
```

```
    string(8) "Anderson"
}
```

In PHP, the var_dump() function is super useful as it outputs variables, its contents, and its content types. Notice that in this case, var_dump($person) is telling us that we have an array, and said array has two elements. These two elements in the array are strings. We also notice that the first associative element (["firSt"]) looks strange. It has a capital "S" in the middle. So, let's make the correction and remove our debugging code. Our code should now look like this:

```php
<?php //buggy_code.php
$person['first'] = 'Thomas';
$person['last'] = 'Anderson';
echo "Hi {$person['first']} {$person['last']}";
```

We run it once more in our shell:

```
php buggy_code.php
```

It returns the following output:

```
Hi Thomas Anderson
```

While this might not be the best debugging tool, it certainly is a very straightforward way to debug code in PHP. I personally am quite fond of this function as it was the very first function I used to debug in my life. Additionally, this is an oversimplified example, but in essence portrays real scenarios, especially when you debug during web development as sometimes you don't know what is being sent to your script. If you are more interested in this function, you should take a look at the function's documentation page: https://www.php.net/manual/en/function.var-dump.php.

You may also want to take a look at the print_r() and var_export() functions.

In Ruby, we don't really have a var_dump() function, but instead, every object has a method already available called inspect(). The inspect() method converts the contents of an object to a string and returns it. Let's redo the same example but in Ruby. Let's create a file called buggy_code.rb and add the following code:

```ruby
# buggy_code.rb
person = Hash.new
person['firSt'] = 'Thomas'
person['last'] = 'Anderson'
print "Hi #{person['first']} #{person['last']}"
```

Let's say we were to run this script on our shell with the following:

```
ruby buggy_code.rb
```

We would get the following output:

```
Hi   Anderson
```

We know ahead of time what the error is, but for educational purposes, let's debug the `person` object by adding the following to our code so that it will now look like this:

```ruby
# buggy_code.rb
person = Hash.new
person['firSt'] = 'Thomas'
person['last'] = 'Anderson'
#print "Hi #{person['first']} #{person['last']}"
print person.inspect
```

We run this script on the shell with the following:

```
ruby buggy_code.rb
```

This will return the following:

```
{"firSt"=>"Thomas", "last"=>"Anderson"}
```

While we could accomplish the same effect by just using `print()`, this is only true because we're analyzing the contents of a hash in this example. If the previous example had a class object, the `print()` function would not show us all of the contents of an object. The `inspect()` method is more generic as it outputs the contents of any type of object.

Since we already know the fix, we can just go ahead and fix the example. Our code should now look like this:

```ruby
# buggy_code.rb
person = Hash.new
person['first'] = 'Thomas'
person['last'] = 'Anderson'
print "Hi #{person['first']} #{person['last']}"
```

Lastly, we can run it again just to verify that our script runs correctly by running this on the shell:

```
ruby buggy_code.rb
```

This would return the following:

```
Hi Thomas Anderson
```

And with this, we've learned a very PHP-esque way to debug scripts. Fortunately, we are not going further down this road. Instead, let's take a look into other more Ruby-esque ways to debug.

Gems for debugging

As you probably guessed, the Ruby community came across the debugging problem just like any other programming community and thus has come up with libraries (or gems) to encapsulate different debug behaviors. We'll talk specifically about three gems that make your debugging experience a whole different path than just dumping values in your code:

- Debug

- Pry

- Byebug

All of these gems were designed for the same purpose, but each one has its own peculiarities and it will depend on your own preference which one you choose to use in your projects. Let's start by looking at the first one.

The debug gem

This gem comes as a replacement (and improvement) to the traditional `lib/debug.rb` standard library. While there are various ways to use this gem, let's start by installing our gem and creating a simple debuggable example. First, we will have to do some setup. Let's use a Gemfile, which we learned about in previous chapters. In an empty folder, create a file called `Gemfile` and add the following code to it:

```
# Gemfile
gem "debug", ">= 1.0.0"
```

Next, we are going to install the gems listed in this file by running the following command within our shell:

```
bundle install
```

This should output something similar to this:

```
Resolving dependencies...
Using bundler 2.4.6
Using debug 1.7.1
Bundle complete! 1 Gemfile dependency, 2 gems now installed.
Use `bundle info [gemname]` to see where a bundled gem is installed.
```

And with this, we have installed the debug gem in our system. Now let's test it out. To save time, you should download the example from the GitHub repo:

```
https://github.com/PacktPublishing/From-PHP-to-Ruby-on-Rails/blob/
main/chapter06/debuggable_example.rb
```

You can also type the whole code, though I wouldn't recommend it as it contains a very long string:

```ruby
# debuggable_example.rb
require 'digest'

user = Hash.new
user['name'] = 'admin'
user['password'] = 'secret'
SECRET_SHA2_PASSWORD =
'32b363908ba2382c892800589d6aa3104dc41e6789d2d6a12512c34ec0632834'
user_sha2_input = Digest::SHA2.hexdigest(user['password'])

if user_sha2_input == SECRET_SHA2_PASSWORD
  print "Your password is CORRECT"
else
  print "Your password is INCORRECT"
end
```

The preceding code may seem a bit complicated at first, but for now, let's focus on running it and the output, and we will explain the outcome of the script.

Let's run our code from the shell with the following:

```
ruby debuggable_example.rb
```

This will output the following:

```
Your password is INCORRECT
```

Our code is basically ciphering a password with an algorithm called SHA2 and compares it to an already ciphered string with the same algorithm. We use the digest module, which we import at the beginning of the file, to cipher the password with Digest::SHA2. If the passwords match, we should get the message Your password is CORRECT. However, we can infer from the output that the passwords do not match. To debug, instead of printing values here and there with the print() function, let's use the debug gem. Since we already installed the gem, we can just import said gem into our script. Let's do that. Let's add the require statement to our third line of code so that the first four lines of code now look like this:

```ruby
# debuggable_example.rb
require 'digest'
require 'debug'
user = Hash.new
...
```

Now that the gem has been imported, we can now create a breakpoint. A breakpoint is a line of code that is taken by a debugger program to pause the execution and let us analyze a program within that specific line of code. It'll be more clear once we try it out. So, let's add a breakpoint right after the hash value for name that has been set. Our code should now look like this:

```
# debuggable_example.rb
require 'digest'
require 'debug'
user = Hash.new
user['name'] = 'admin'
user['password'] = 'secret'
SECRET_SHA2_PASSWORD =
'32b363908ba2382c892800589d6aa3104dc41e6789d2d6a12512c34ec0632834'
binding.break
user_sha2_input = Digest::SHA2.hexdigest(user['password'])
if user_sha2_input == SECRET_SHA2_PASSWORD
  print "Your password is CORRECT"
else
  print "Your password is INCORRECT"
end
```

Now, let's run our script just like any other script:

```
ruby debuggable_example.rb
```

But you'll notice something new. Our script will now result in a pause in the middle of the execution. Instead of outputting the text, our shell will now look like this:

```
[4, 13] in debuggable_example.rb
      4|
      5| user = Hash.new
      6| user['name'] = 'admin'
      7| user['password'] = 'admin'
      8| SECRET_SHA2_PASSWORD = '32b3639…'
=>    9| binding.break
     10| user_sha2_input = Digest::SHA2.hexdigest
         (user['password'])
     11|
     12| if user_sha2_input == SECRET_SHA2_PASSWORD
     13|   print "Your password is CORRECT"
=>#0  <main> at debuggable_example.rb:9
(rdbg)
```

I've truncated the ciphered value (`'32b3639…'`), but on your screen, it should show the full value. Notice how the execution has paused. What sorcery is this? Nothing other than the debug gem in action. And we can now even test things out. For example, let's see what's inside of the user hash. Within our debug shell, let's type the following:

```
user
```

Right after pressing *Enter*, the shell will return the value that has been assigned to `user`:

```
(rdbg) user
{"name"=>"admin", "password"=>"secret"}
(rdbg)
```

Notice how our `user` variable has both `name` and `password` indexes. But what would happen if we tried to get the value of the `user_sha2_input` variable? Let's do it. On the debug shell, type the following:

```
user_sha2_input
```

This returns an empty value:

```
(ruby) user_sha2_input
nil
(rdbg)
```

This is because the program has not yet reached the code where that variable is set. However, this special shell is already providing useful information by showing us all sorts of data related to the execution, such as what script we are running (`debuggable_example.rb`), and what line we are currently at (`=> 9| binding.break`). We can also interact with this shell. Let's type `next` and then press *Enter*:

```
(rdbg) next
```

This will move forward in the breakpoint one line at a time. The shell will re-render again so that it now displays the following:

```
[5, 14] in debuggable_example.rb
    5| user = Hash.new
    6| user['name'] = 'admin'
    7| user['password'] = 'admin'
    8| SECRET_SHA2_PASSWORD = '32b3639…'
    9| binding.break
=> 10| user_sha2_input = Digest::SHA2.hexdigest
       (user['password'])
   11|
   12| if user_sha2_input == SECRET_SHA2_PASSWORD
```

```
    13|    print "Your password is CORRECT"
    14| else
=>#0  <main> at debuggable_example.rb:10
 (rdbg)
```

Notice that we moved from line 9 to line 10. Let's move one more line of code so that we allow the program to assign the password. This time we will use the shortcut for next, which is just the first letter, n:

```
(rdbg) n
```

As it renders yet again, we now see that our breakpoint has moved to the if statement:

```
[5, 14] in debuggable_example.rb
     5| user = Hash.new
     6| user['name'] = 'admin'
     7| binding.break
     8| user['password'] = 'admin'
     9|
=>  10| if user_sha2_input == SECRET_SHA2_PASSWORD
    11|    print "Your password is CORRECT"
    12| else
    13|    print "Your password is INCORRECT"
    14| end
=>#0  <main> at debuggable_example.rb:10
 (rdbg)
```

Now we can view the contents of the password. Again, let's type the user_sha2_input variable in this debugging shell:

```
(rdbg) user_sha2_input
```

We confirm that the value is now there, as the output is now the following:

```
(rdbg) user_sha2_input
2bb80d537b1da3e38bd30361aa855686bde0eacd7162fef6a25fe97bf527a25b
 (rdbg)
```

This is where our shell becomes extremely handy. We can test the if clause prior to executing it. Let's copy the if clause, but without the if keyword, and paste it into the debug shell:

```
user_sha2_input == SECRET_SHA2_PASSWORD
```

This returns what the if sentence is evaluating:

```
false
```

Apparently, someone changed the password to our script but made a mistake. You see, the problem with the SHA2 algorithm is that it's not an encryption algorithm that you can encrypt and decrypt so that you can get the original value. SHA2 is a hashing algorithm, which means that you are only able to cipher a value. If you need to use it for a password, then what you do is save this ciphered value and compare it to the user's ciphered input. That way, not even the program has the original password, thus protecting the user's password even from the program itself. In this case, we can quickly confirm that the passwords don't match. Let's debug this issue. Let's compare ciphered values. First, let's output the `user_sha2_input` value:

```
user_sha2_input
```

This returns the following:

```
2bb80d537b1da3e38bd30361aa855686bde0eacd7162fef6a25fe97bf527a25b
```

And if we compare it to the `SECRET_SHA2_PASSWORD` value from our code, we see the following:

```
32b363908ba2382c892800589d6aa3104dc41e6789d2d6a12512c34ec0632834
```

Seeing them close to each other, we can easily see just from the first four digits that they have different values. But before we fix our code, let's finish our script's execution with the `continue` debug command by typing it into the debug shell:

```
(rdbg) continue
```

This will continue our script's execution until it either finds another breakpoint (of which there are no more in this case) or until it reaches the end of the program (as in this case). Additionally, it will output the same text as the first time we ran our script:

```
(rdbg) continue    # command
Your password is INCORRECT
```

Now the shell is back to normal, we can get on to fixing the issue. Unfortunately, there is no way to get the original password (at least not until quantum computers are available to us). Fortunately, we already have the correct value from our previous debug session:

```
2bb80d537b1da3e38bd30361aa855686bde0eacd7162fef6a25fe97bf527a25b
```

We can just copy this value into our `SECRET_SHA2_PASSWORD` variable and remove the breakpoint, so our code now looks like this:

```
# debuggable_example.rb
require 'digest'
require 'debug'
user = Hash.new
user['name'] = 'admin'
```

```
user['password'] = 'secret'
SECRET_SHA2_PASSWORD =
'2bb80d537b1da3e38bd30361aa855686bde0eacd7162fef6a25fe97bf527a25b'
user_sha2_input = Digest::SHA2.hexdigest(user['password'])

if user_sha2_input == SECRET_SHA2_PASSWORD
  print "Your password is CORRECT"
else
  print "Your password is INCORRECT"
end
```

Let's run it once more to confirm that the fix is correct by typing this in our shell:

```
ruby debuggable_example.rb
```

The output should be the following:

```
Your password is CORRECT
```

With this, we have successfully debugged our script with the debug gem. As we previously saw, with the debug gem, we can run a script line by line, and add more than one break point, and that was just a simple example. I recommend you play around with this gem more and take a peek at other commands that the gem supports: https://github.com/ruby/debug.

The pry gem

The debug gem is only one of the options that we have available to debug our code nowadays. The second gem we are going to take a look at for debugging is the pry gem. As its name clearly suggests, pry is a a gem that spawns an interactive console that is able to observe deep within a Ruby program. From its GitHub page, we get that pry is an attempt to replace the classic **Interactive Ruby** (or **IRB**). Though it has its similarities with the debug gem, it does have its own approach to the debug paradigm. Let's take it out for a test drive so you can see what I'm talking about. We'll start by simply installing the gem by running the following command on our command shell:

```
gem install pry
```

We should see the following output:

```
Fetching pry-0.14.2.gem
Successfully installed pry-0.14.2
Parsing documentation for pry-0.14.2
Installing ri documentation for pry-0.14.2
Done installing documentation for pry after 0 seconds
1 gem installed
```

Now you can either download the example from `https://github.com/PacktPublishing/From-PHP-to-Ruby-on-Rails/blob/main/chapter06/pryable_example.rb` or simply type the code. The file we either download or create should be named `pryable_example.rb` and it looks like this:

```ruby
# pryable_example.rb
class Person
  attr_accessor :first_name, :last_name
  def full_name
    puts "#{first_name}#{last_name}"
  end
end


person = Person.new
person.first_name = "Zach"
person.last_name = "Smith"
person.full_name
```

Now let's execute the script we just created from the shell:

```
ruby pryable_example.rb
```

It should output just a name:

```
ZachSmith
```

Of course, we made a typo on purpose (failing to include a space between the name and last name), but now let's see the pry magic. Let's import `pry` and add a breakpoint. Our code should now look like this:

```ruby
# pryable_example.rb
require 'pry'
class Person
  attr_accessor :first_name, :last_name
  def full_name
    puts "#{first_name}#{last_name}"
  end
end


person = Person.new
person.first_name = "Zach"
person.last_name = "Smith"
binding.pry
person.full_name
```

Let's run our script again:

```
ruby pryable_example.rb
```

And, just like the debug gem, we will also enter an interactive shell:

```
        9: end
       10:
       11: person = Person.new
       12: person.first_name = "Zach"
       13: person.last_name = "Smith"
 =>    14: binding.pry
       15: person.full_name
 [1]  pry(main)>
```

What we must consider here is that the commands are going to be different. We will start with a simple command within this shell. Let's type `ls` (that's a lowercase L and a lowercase S), just like the Linux command:

```
ls
```

The prompt will return something like this:

```
 [6]  pry(main)> ls
self.methods: inspect   to_s
locals:  _   __   _dir_   _ex_   _file_   _in_   _out_   person
pry_instance
 [7]  pry(main)>
```

Pry lists the content (in memory) from our program, and pry lists it as if it were a filesystem. If we wanted to "pry" into the `person` object, we could navigate as if it were a folder. Let's do that with the following command:

```
cd person
```

And right after that, let's do an `ls` again:

```
ls
```

Now the prompt will show the contents of `person`:

```
 [7]  pry(main)> cd person
 [8]  pry(#<Person>):1> ls
Person#methods: first_name   first_name=   full_name   last_name   last_
name=
self.methods: __pry__
instance variables: @first_name   @last_name
```

```
locals: _  __  _dir_  _ex_  _file_  _in_  _out_
  pry_instance
[9] pry(#<Person>):1>
```

Depending on the version of Ruby that you may have installed, you may see the previous prompt or a similar one with slight variations, but one way or another they will all show the contents of the person object. If we closely take a look, we see the first_name, last_name, and full_name methods in addition to the @first_name and @last_name variables. That is one of the advantages of pry as it allows us to dig deep into an object. Another useful thing we can do is fix and reload our code, which simply means that we can change part of the code and then reload it into memory without having to stop the current execution. If we go to our source code, and we fix line seven by adding a space between first_name and last_name, our code should now look like this:

```
# pryable_example.rb
require 'pry'
class Person
  attr_accessor :first_name, :last_name
  def full_name
    puts "#{first_name} #{last_name}"
  end
end

person = Person.new
person.first_name = "Zach"
person.last_name = "Smith"
binding.pry
person.full_name
```

Lastly, while still in our interactive shell, we run this command:

reload-method

This should make the prompt show us where our breakpoint is again:

```
    9: end
   10:
   11: person = Person.new
   12: person.first_name = "Zach"
   13: person.last_name = "Smith"
=> 14: binding.pry
   15: person.full_name
```

Now let's get the full name again by typing the following:

```
person.full_name
```

We then see the fixed full name in the output:

```
[1] pry(main)> person.full_name
Zach Smith
=> nil
[2] pry(main)>
```

We can now exit the debug shell with pry's exit alias (! ! !):

```
!!!
```

This exits the debug shell. So, as you can see, we have a lot of advantages, such as the level of depth of our view of the object. However, we do have a major downside. With pry, we can only see the contents of that specific moment of execution. We cannot move to another line of code as with debug. What we can do is add multiple breakpoints as pry allows it. Either way, don't let that downside deter you from trying it out.

The byebug gem

And yet another tool that is available for us is the byebug gem. Byebug is another debugger that does not depend on internal core sources. It works in a similar manner to the two options that we've previously reviewed. Additionally, the gem has support for popular IDEs such as Sublime, Atom, and VS Code.

Let's take a quick dive into this tool. We are going to install the byebug gem. On a shell, type the following command:

```
gem install byebug
```

We should see the following output on our shell:

```
Fetching byebug-11.1.3.gem
Building native extensions. This could take a while...
Successfully installed byebug-11.1.3
Parsing documentation for byebug-11.1.3
Installing ri documentation for byebug-11.1.3
Done installing documentation for byebug after 4 seconds
1 gem installed
```

Now that the gem is available, let's create a file called byeable_example.rb with the following content:

```ruby
# byeable_example.rb
require 'byebug'

[1,5,7,9].each do |index|
  not_label = index ? "NOT":""
  output = "#{index} is #{not_label} larger than 6"
```

```
    puts output
  end
```

Let's first run our program without any breakpoints. In our shell, let's type this:

ruby byeable_example.rb

The output will be the following:

```
1 is NOT larger than 6
5 is NOT larger than 6
7 is NOT larger than 6
9 is NOT larger than 6
```

Our program is showing the same message for every number, which is not what is intended. Since our gem is already installed and loaded, we only need to add a breakpoint. And we do that by adding the byebug text. Let's add that to our code right before the output variable is printed. Our code should now look like this:

```
# byeable_example.rb
require 'byebug'

[1,5,7,9].each do |index|
  not_label = index ? "NOT":""
  output = "#{index} is #{not_label} larger than 6"
  byebug
  puts output
end
```

And again, let's run our script in the shell:

ruby byeable_example.rb

As with the other debuggers, we see our shell change into an interactive debugging shell:

```
    1: # byeable_example.rb
    2: require 'byebug'
    3:
    4: [1,5,7,9].each do |index|
    5:   not_label = index ? "NOT":""
    6:   output = "#{index} is #{not_label} larger than 6"
    7:   byebug
=>  8:   puts output
    9: end
  (byebug)
```

From this shell, we can write commands and see the contents of variables, just like we did with debugger and pry. We see the file and the breakpoint that we defined on line 7. At this point, we have access to the index variable. Let's type this into the byebug shell:

```
index
```

We immediately see the value of this variable:

```
1
```

As we are inside an each loop, the value for the index variable has been populated by the first value from the array ([1,5,7,9]), which in this case is 1. We can also view what's inside the not_label variable. Let's type it on the byebug shell:

```
not_label
```

Now we see the contents of said variable:

```
"NOT"
```

This is because the not_label variable is taking the index value and instead of comparing it to 6, we are just passing it to the ternary operator (the ? symbol), ergo the not_label variable will always have the text "NOT" as its value. We can verify this by typing the keyword continue:

```
continue
```

The continue command will carry on the execution of the program until it finds another breakpoint. As we are inside a loop, we will move on to the next element in the array, until we reach the breakpoint again. Let's see what's inside the index value again in the shell:

```
index
```

This will output the following:

```
5
```

That confirms that we've moved to the next element in the array. Let's see what's inside of the not_label variable again:

```
not_label
```

We should see the same value:

```
"NOT"
```

This will happen with every value assigned to the `index` variable. So let's exit by typing the `exit` command on the byebug shell:

```
exit
```

Our shell should go back to normal. Now let's fix our code by adding a comparison inside our `not_label` variable and removing our breakpoint. Our code should look like this:

```
# byeable_example.rb
require 'byebug'

[1,5,7,9].each do |index|
  not_label = index < 6 ? "NOT":""
  output = "#{index} is #{not_label} larger than 6"
  puts output
end
```

Now let's do a final run of our script:

```
ruby byeable_example.rb
```

This should correctly output the text messages:

```
1 is NOT larger than 6
5 is NOT larger than 6
7 is  larger than 6
9 is  larger than 6
```

Congrats! Our code has been debugged and fixed. Again, this is a vastly simplified example, but I hope you get the idea of how useful byebug is. Byebug has additional commands, configuration options, and even a historical log of our commands. Please take a look at byebug's GitHub page for more information: `https://github.com/deivid-rodriguez/byebug`.

As you probably noticed, all of these gems work in a very similar manner. As we'll see in the next section, this is because they are all built based on IRB.

Understanding IRB's usefulness

In *Chapter 3*, we briefly saw the **IRB** shell, and I hope you noticed some of the similarities between IRB and our debugging tools. Basically, what these gems do is enhance IRB so that we can view variables in memory, move around execution points, and work in a "frozen" state of our program. At the end of the day, you will be able to choose which one of these tools is more convenient for your everyday use. I could steer you toward one, or you could simply use the built-in IRB. One technique I saw a fellow developer use was that he wrote most of his code in IRB, and once the code ran without problems, he would just copy the code from IRB into an IDE to save his work. This saved him a lot of time that he would have otherwise used on testing. Another coworker used a very popular IDE called RubyMine. This tool allows us to add breaking points at the touch of a button (among many other features). Additionally, one downside of using debuggers is that you add debug code when setting up breakpoints. This could potentially break your code if you forget to remove the breakpoints when you commit your code into your code base. RubyMine removes that risk as breakpoints are not added to your code but rather managed by the IDE.

Nowadays, most IDEs have integrated some sort of debugger mechanism for your convenience. As that might be outside of the scope of this book, you might want to check those IDEs and their own implementation of debugging on your own:

- `https://www.sublimetext.com/`
- `https://code.visualstudio.com/`
- `https://www.jetbrains.com/ruby/`

Whatever path you take is entirely up to you. I just wanted to give you an understanding of what IRB is, and how powerful it can be in Ruby development.

PHP programmers who come from a Laravel background will be familiar with the tinker tool, which is basically an interactive shell for PHP with Laravel components loaded. I must admit that tinker (`https://github.com/laravel/tinker`) looks a lot like a tool that Ruby on Rails has: the Rails console. The Rails console is basically IRB with Ruby on Rails components loaded for ease of use. But let's not get ahead of ourselves. We first must learn about Ruby on Rails.

Summary

In this chapter, we learned about the different functions we can use to debug in PHP and the equivalent in Ruby, and how to debug our code by using three different tools that are easily configured and installed. While not wanting to impose my debugging gem of choice, I will say that for several years I used pry, until byebug came along. I suggest you not only try byebug but also be on the lookout for new debugging gems. We also learned how to add breakpoints to our debug code and how useful and powerful these breakpoints can be during development. Lastly, we learned that all of these gems are basically enhanced IRBs, so we can easily use any of them as they all behave in a very similar fashion.

Having seen all this, we are now ready to board the Ruby on Rails wagon.

Part 2:
Ruby and the Web

In this part, you will get an introduction to how Ruby is used in web development through the most popular Ruby framework, Ruby on Rails. In addition to this, you will learn the basics of database handling and views, and finally, get an overview of the differences in hosting for Ruby on Rails applications in comparison to PHP applications.

This part has the following chapters:

- *Chapter 7, Understanding Convention over Configuration*
- *Chapter 8, Models, DBs, and Active Record*
- *Chapter 9, Bringing It All Together*
- *Chapter 10, Considerations for Hosting Rails Applications versus PHP Applications*

7
Understanding Convention over Configuration

Convention over configuration is a phrase you'll encounter more often than not once we start using Ruby on Rails. Yes, you read that right – we are ready to start using one of the fondest web frameworks for Ruby developers. And while it's fun, we do need to understand the structure and how the Ruby on Rails configuration works before we start doing our programming.

In this chapter, we will cover installing Ruby on Rails and its file structure so that we can move around the framework with ease. Once we understand where to place things, we will move on to using a framework with the MVC paradigm. Lastly, we will learn how to send and receive data with forms and sessions.

With the Ruby on Rails configuration in mind, in this chapter, we will cover the following topics:

- Installing Ruby on Rails
- Ruby on Rails file structure
- The MVC implementation of Ruby on Rails
- User interaction with Ruby on Rails

Technical requirements

To follow along with this chapter, we will need the following:

- Any IDE to view/edit code (SublimeText, Visual Studio Code, Notepad++, Vim, Emacs, and so on)
- For macOS users, you will also need to have XCode Command Line Tools installed
- Ruby version 2.6 installed and ready to use
- Git client installed on our local machine

The code presented in this chapter is available at `https://github.com/PacktPublishing/From-PHP-to-Ruby-on-Rails/`.

If there is Ruby magic, there is Rails magic

By this point, you're probably familiar with what is fondly referred to as Ruby magic. We saw some examples where Ruby "magically" generates output out of syntax that simply makes sense, but we didn't know exactly how it's done (hint: meta-programming). In the same fashion, Ruby on Rails (also known as Rails or simply RoR) internally uses meta-programming to generate functionality that is not explicitly for our eyes to see. We'll understand it by looking at more examples, but first, we need to install Ruby on Rails.

Installing Ruby on Rails

Just like the libraries we've seen so far, Rails is an open source gem. It behaves a little differently than the gems we've seen so far as it uses many dependencies and can generate code examples, but at the end of the day, it's still a gem. This means that we can either install it by itself, or we can include it in a Gemfile. For this section, we will have to divide the process into three separate sections – macOS installation, Windows installation, and Linux installation – as each operating system behaves differently.

Installing Ruby on Rails on macOS

The first step of setting up our local environment is to install `rbenv`. For most Mac installations, `brew` will simplify this process. Let's get started with the steps:

1. Let's open a shell and run the following command:

    `brew install rbenv`

2. This should install the `rbenv` program. Now, you'll need to add the following line to your bash profile:

    `eval "$(rbenv init -)"`

3. Once you've added this line to your profile, you should activate the change by either opening a new shell or running the following command:

    `source ~/.bash_profile`

    Note that this command may differ if you're using another shell, such as zsh or fish.

4. With `rbenv` installed, we need to install Ruby `2.6.10` with the following command:

    `rbenv install 2.6.10`

5. Once Ruby 2.6.10 has been installed, we must set the default Ruby version with the following command:

    ```
    rbenv global 2.6.10
    ```

6. Now, we need to install the program to manage gems, called `bundler`. Let's install it with the following command:

    ```
    gem install bundler
    ```

With that, our environment is ready for the next steps in this chapter.

If you wish to see more details about this installation, please refer to the following web page: `https://www.digitalocean.com/community/tutorials/how-to-install-ruby-on-rails-with-rbenv-on-macos`.

Installing Ruby on Rails on Windows

Follow these steps to install Ruby on Rails on Windows:

1. To set up our local environment, first, we must install Git for Windows. We can download the package from `https://gitforwindows.org/`.

    Once downloaded, we can run the installer; it should open the installer application:

Figure 7.1 – Git installer

You can safely accept the default options unless you want to change any of the specific behavior from Git. At the end of the installation process, you may just deselect all the options of the wizard and move on to the next step:

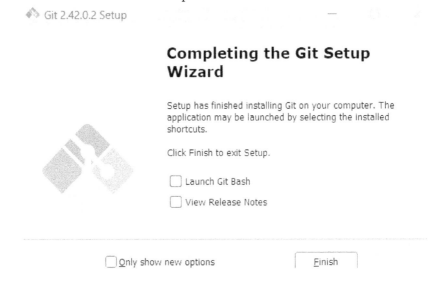

Figure 7.2 – Git finalized installation

We will also need the Git SDK installed for some dependencies that Ruby on Rails requires. We can get the installer from `https://github.com/git-for-windows/build-extra/releases/tag/git-sdk-1.0.8`.

Be careful and select the correct option for your platform (32 or 64 bits). In my case, I had to choose 64 bits, so I downloaded the **git-sdk-installer-1.0.8.0-64.7z.exe** binary:

Figure 7.3 – Git SDK download

2. Once this package has been downloaded, run it; we will be asked where we want the Git SDK to be installed. The default option is fine (`C:\git-sdk-64`):

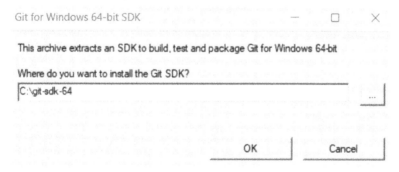

Figure 7.4 – Git SDK installation location

This package might take a while to complete as it has to download other additional packages but it will do so on its own. Please be patient. Once this package has finished installing the SDK, it will open a Git Bash console, which looks similar to Windows PowerShell. We can close this Git Bash console window and open another Windows PowerShell.

3. Once we have the new window open, we must type the following command:

    ```
    new-item -type file -path $profile -force
    ```

    This command will help us create a Windows PowerShell profile, which will allow us to execute commands every time we open a Windows PowerShell console. Once we've run the previous command, we may also close the Windows PowerShell window, and move on to the next step. At this point, we will install `rbenv`, which allows us to install multiple versions of Ruby. However, this program wasn't created for Windows, so its installation is a little different than in other operating systems.

4. Let's open a browser and go to the *rbenv for Windows* web page: `https://github.com/ccmywish/rbenv-for-windows`.

    On that page, we will find instructions on how to install `rbenv`, which we will do now.

5. Let's open a new Windows PowerShell and type the following command:

    ```
    $env:RBENV_ROOT = "C:\Ruby-on-Windows "
    ```

    This command will set a special environment variable that will be used for the `rbenv` installation.

6. Once we've run this command, we must download the rest of the required files with the following command:

    ```
    iwr -useb "https://github.com/ccmywish/rbenv-for-windows/raw/
    main/tools/install.ps1" | iex
    ```

7. Once this command has finished downloading the files from GitHub, modify the user's profile with the following command from within the Windows PowerShell:

    ```
    notepad $profile
    ```

    This will open the Notepad application and the profile we previously set.

8. On the `rbenv-for-windows` web page, we can see what the content of the file should be. Let's add it with Notepad so that the profile file now looks like this:

    ```
    $env:RBENV_ROOT = "C:\Ruby-on-Windows"
    & "$env:RBENV_ROOT\rbenv\bin\rbenv.ps1" init
    ```

    Save and close Notepad, and close all Windows PowerShell windows that we may have open. We should open a new Windows PowerShell to make these changes take effect. As this is the first time `rbenv` is running, our console will automatically install a default Ruby version. This might take a while and will put our patience to the test. Once the process has finished, we should see an output similar to this one:

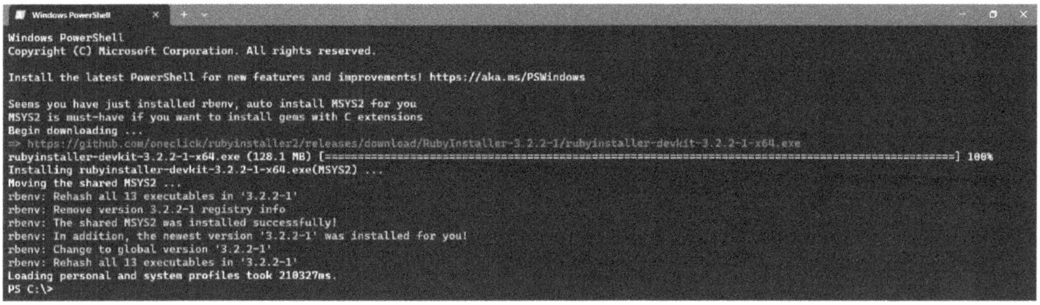

Figure 7.5 – rbenv post-installation script

Now, we are ready to install other versions of Ruby. For Ruby on Rails 5, we will install Ruby 2.6.10.

9. Let's install it by running the following command on the same Windows Powershell window that we just opened:

```
rbenv install 2.6.10
```

The program will ask us whether we want to install the Lite version or the Full version. Choose the Full version. Once again, this might take a while, so please be patient.

10. Once this command has finished running, we must set this Ruby version for our whole system. We can do this by running the following command:

```
rbenv global 2.6.10
```

11. To confirm that this version of Ruby has been installed and enabled, use the following command:

```
ruby --version
```

This should give us the following output:

```
ruby 2.6.10-1 (set by C: \Ruby-on-Windows \global.txt)
```

12. Ruby needs a program called `bundler` to manage all the dependencies on our system. So, let's install this program with the following command:

```
gem install bundler
```

13. Once this gem has been installed, we must update the RubyGem system with the following command:

```
gem update --system 3.2.3
```

This command will also take a while to compute, but once it's finished, we will be ready to use Ruby on Rails on Windows.

Next, let's see the steps for installing Ruby on Rails on Linux.

Installing Ruby on Rails on Linux

For Ubuntu and Debian Linux distributions, we must also install `rbenv` and the dependencies necessary for Ruby on Rails to run correctly:

1. Let's start by opening a terminal and running the following command:

   ```
   sudo apt update
   ```

2. Once this command has finished updating `apt`, we must install our dependencies for Ruby, Ruby on Rails, and some gems that require compiling. We'll do so by running the following command:

   ```
   sudo apt install git curl libssl-dev libreadline-dev zlib1g-
   dev autoconf bison build-essential libyaml-dev libreadline-dev
   libncurses5-dev libffi-dev libgdbm-dev pkg-config sqlite3 nodejs
   ```

3. This command might take a while. Once it has finished running, we can install `rbenv` with the following command:

   ```
   curl -fsSL https://github.com/rbenv/rbenv-installer/raw/HEAD/
   bin/rbenv-installer | bash
   ```

4. We should add `rbenv` to our `$PATH`. Let's do so by running the following command:

   ```
   echo 'export PATH="$HOME/.rbenv/bin:$PATH"' >> ~/.bashrc
   ```

5. Now, let's add the initialize command for `rbenv` to our bash profile with the following command:

   ```
   echo 'eval "$(rbenv init -)"' >> ~/.bashrc
   ```

6. Next, run the bash profile with the following command:

   ```
   source ~/.bashrc
   ```

7. This command will (among other things) make the `rbenv` executable available to us. Now, we can install Ruby 2.6.10 on our system with the following command:

   ```
   rbenv install 2.6.10
   ```

8. This command might take a little while as it installs `openssl` and that process will take some time. Once this command has finished installing Ruby 2.6.10, we need to set it as the default Ruby version for the whole machine. We can do so by running the following command:

   ```
   rbenv global 2.6.10
   ```

9. We can confirm that this version of Ruby has been installed by running the following command:

   ```
   ruby --version
   ```

This will result in the following output:

```
ruby 2.6.10p210 (2022-04-12 revision 67958) [x86_64-linux]
```

10. Ruby needs a program called `bundler` to manage all the dependencies on our system. So, let's install this program with the following command:

```
gem install bundler
```

11. Once this gem has been installed, we can update the RubyGems system with the following command:

```
gem update --system 3.2.3
```

This command will also take a while to compute, but once it's finished, we will be ready to use Ruby on Rails on Linux.

For other Linux distributions and other operating systems, please refer to the official Ruby-lang page: `https://www.ruby-lang.org/en/documentation/installation/`.

Downloading our Ruby on Rails application

While there are a couple of ways to use Rails code, for ease of use, we will download an existing project as an example. We'll use the Git tool to clone the project. Open a terminal and type the following command:

```
git clone https://github.com/PacktPublishing/From-PHP-to-Ruby-on-
Rails.git
```

This will generate a folder called `From-PHP-to-Ruby-on-Rails`. Now, let's navigate into the project folder with the following command:

```
cd From-PHP-to-Ruby-on-Rails/chapter07/rails5/
```

Once we've navigated into this folder, you'll notice a `Gemfile`. If we open that `Gemfile` with our IDE of choice, we'll see the beginning of the dependencies:

```
source 'https://rubygems.org'
git_source(:github) do |repo_name|
  repo_name = "#{repo_name}/#{repo_name}"
    unless repo_name.include?("/")
  "https://github.com/#{repo_name}.git"
end
# Bundle edge Rails instead: gem 'rails', github:
  'rails/rails'
gem 'rails', '~> 5.1.7'
...
```

Let's not dwell on all the details (yet) except for the Rails gem that is declared there. As you may recall from the previous chapters, we can install gems and their dependencies using the `bundle` command. So, let's do just that. Type the following command:

```
bundle install
```

The `bundle` command takes all of the gems declared in `Gemfile`, creates a dependency map (called `Gemfile.lock`), and installs these dependencies. The output of this command should look similar to this:

```
Fetching gem metadata from https://rubygems.org/...........
Resolving dependencies...
Using rake 13.0.6
Using concurrent-ruby 1.2.2
Using minitest 5.18.1
...
Using rails 5.1.7
Using sass-rails 5.0.7
Bundle complete! 16 Gemfile dependencies, 79 gems now installed.
Use `bundle info [gemname]` to see where a bundled gem is installed.
```

The output has been truncated for brevity. To prove that our dependencies have been installed correctly, we should run the following command:

```
bundle exec rails --version
```

We should obtain the version of Rails that we just installed:

```
Rails 5.1.7
```

And voilá – we have successfully installed Ruby on Rails. However, there are still a couple of things we need to clarify before we can start using this framework. Firstly, you may be wondering why we used the `bundle exec rails --version` command and not just `rails --version`. Well, as the Rails developers have to deal with Rails being able to run in different environments and platforms (be it Windows, Linux, macOS, and others), one way to make sure the "bundle" of libraries works correctly is to run rails commands in the context of the "bundle." This is just a fancy way of saying it's for "running the command using the libraries we just installed." So, from now on, all of our Rails commands will be wrapped with the `bundle exec` command. If you're interested in more details regarding this command, please refer to `https://bundler.io/v2.4/man/bundle-exec.1.html`.

Now that we've finally installed Ruby on Rails, we'll start our server and take a ride on the Rails.

Starting our Ruby on Rails project

Running our sample Rails application requires that we run the following command:

```
bundle exec rails server
```

We should see the following output after pressing the *Enter* key:

```
=> Booting Puma
=> Rails 5.1.7 application starting in development
=> Run `rails server -h` for more startup options
Puma starting in single mode...
* Version 3.12.6 (ruby 2.6.10-p210), codename: Llamas in
  Pajamas
* Min threads: 5, max threads: 5
* Environment: development
* Listening on tcp://localhost:3000
Use Ctrl-C to stop
```

Once we see this message, it means that we are ready to rock and roll. Open any web browser and, in the location bar, type the following:

```
http://localhost:3000
```

We should see the following page:

Yay! You're on Rails!

```
Rails version: 5.1.7
Ruby version: 2.6.10 (arm64-darwin22)
```

Figure 7.6 – Rails landing page

Congratulations! We have successfully run our first Ruby on Rails sample application. It's always exciting and magical (at least for me) when you see this image for the first time. And by magic, I mean the way Rails is configured to use a web server and other tools to make this page possible. Now, before we start messing around with this sample application, let's look at the file structure of Ruby on Rails.

Rails file structure explained

One of the first things you need to learn as you learn Ruby on Rails is learning where things go in its file structure. In my case, it took me too long to connect the dots, but once I did, I no longer struggled with placing things. In the long run, it even helps you whenever a new Rails version comes out as the file structures are very similar among versions. So, let's look at all the folders. Here's the file structure:

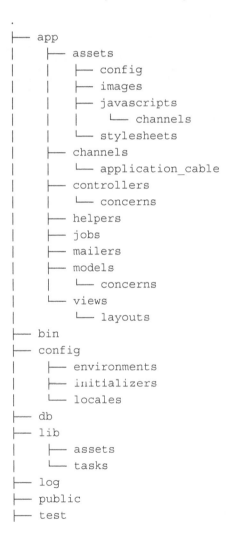

```
.
├── app
│   ├── assets
│   │   ├── config
│   │   ├── images
│   │   ├── javascripts
│   │   │   └── channels
│   │   └── stylesheets
│   ├── channels
│   │   └── application_cable
│   ├── controllers
│   │   └── concerns
│   ├── helpers
│   ├── jobs
│   ├── mailers
│   ├── models
│   │   └── concerns
│   └── views
│       └── layouts
├── bin
├── config
│   ├── environments
│   ├── initializers
│   └── locales
├── db
├── lib
│   ├── assets
│   └── tasks
├── log
├── public
├── test
```

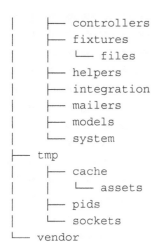

```
|       ├── controllers
|       ├── fixtures
|       |     └── files
|       ├── helpers
|       ├── integration
|       ├── mailers
|       ├── models
|       └── system
├── tmp
|       ├── cache
|       |     └── assets
|       ├── pids
|       └── sockets
└── vendor
```

It may seem like a lot and even overwhelming, but we will be using five folders: `app/controllers`, `app/models`, `app/views`, `config`, and `public`. Rails is a **Model View Controller** (**MVC**) framework, and as such, we can infer that controllers will go into the `controllers` folder, models in the `models` folder, and views in the `views` folder. In the `config` folder, we'll store configuration values such as our defined URL routes, database connection values, and values that may differ from environment to environment (that is, development, production, and testing). Last but not least, in the `public` folder, we'll store certain assets that the web server needs to access. We might occasionally have to handle other folders, but for the most part, as a rookie RoR developer, we will mostly handle the aforementioned folders.

Now that we've taken a peek into the file structure of Rails, we can move on to the next section, where we'll dive into how the MVC pattern comes into play.

MVC at its finest

As mentioned previously, Rails is an MVC controller. If you've used PHP frameworks in the past, such as CodeIgniter, Symfony, or Laravel, you will probably be familiar with the term. If you're not, I recommend checking out these pages:

- `https://www.oracle.com/technical-resources/articles/java/java-se-app-design-with-mvc.html`

- `https://pusher.com/blog/laravel-mvc-use/#why-use-mvc`

In summary, the MVC pattern divides our application into three components – the model, in which we save all of our business logic (mostly but not exclusively by connecting to a database), the view, in which we hold what is to be shown on the browser (HTML for the most part), and the controller, which serves as the organizer of the previous two. If we were to use an example to explain this, a user authentication component would function as follows: the HTML form that shows the user and password fields would be created on the view. Once the user clicks on the button to submit these fields, the controller will receive the form data (user and password), and pass these to the model. After this, the model will connect to the database and attempt to find an entry on the database that matches the user and password. If we find a user entry, the model will send back the user entry found on the database. The next step would be the controller telling the browser to redirect to a page that shows the user as signed in and displays said user data that was passed by the model. While this may sound like a lot of work, Rails does an excellent job of abstracting these components in a way that is almost invisible to us. And this is where we will see how convention over configuration works in Rails. In other frameworks, we may have to define where our controller, model, and views live. We have the liberty to do so. In Rails, however, we need no such distinction. And this works like magic.

Let's consider an example of creating a controller. The simplest way to do so is by using Rails generators. Rails generators are tools that help us generate boilerplate controllers, models, and more. We'll use this tool to generate our controller. Let's go to the terminal where we have our Rails project still running. Within that terminal, press (and keep pressing) the *Ctrl* key. Then (while still pressing the *Ctrl* key) press the *C* key. This will send a signal to our application to stop; the terminal should display something like this:

```
...
^C- Gracefully stopping, waiting for requests to finish
=== puma shutdown: 2023-07-22 21:52:24 -0700 ===
- Goodbye!
Exiting
```

Now, let's generate a Home controller. We can do so by running the following command:

```
bundle exec rails generate controller Home
```

This will output the following:

```
Running via Spring preloader in process 76607
      create    app/controllers/home_controller.rb
      invoke    erb
      create     app/views/home
      invoke    test_unit
      create     test/controllers/home_controller_test.rb
      invoke    helper
      create     app/helpers/home_helper.rb
      invoke     test_unit
```

```
invoke   assets
invoke     coffee
create       app/assets/javascripts/home.coffee
invoke     scss
create       app/assets/stylesheets/home.scss
```

This process will also generate the controller and a couple of other files for testing and formatting; we will ignore them. Let's just focus on the generated controller in app/controllers/home_ controller.rb. Let's look at its contents:

```
class HomeController < ApplicationController
end
```

For now, it's an empty controller, but we will soon populate it with actions that we will map using Rails routes (https://guides.rubyonrails.org/routing.html).

If you're unfamiliar with the concept, the routes file simply maps a specific URL to a controller and an action. In simple terms, this specifies what controller action will be called when a specific URL is called. Let's start by creating a URL that will be called when we open our browser to http:// localhost:3000/home.

So, let's start by starting our application again, but now, instead of using rails server, we'll use the shortcut command, rails s:

```
bundle exec rails s
```

We should see the following output after pressing the *Enter* key:

```
=> Booting Puma
=> Rails 5.1.7 application starting in development
=> Run `rails server -h` for more startup options
Puma starting in single mode...
* Version 3.12.6 (ruby 2.6.10-p210), codename: Llamas in Pajamas
* Min threads: 5, max threads: 5
* Environment: development
* Listening on tcp://localhost:3000
Use Ctrl-C to stop
```

Since we have not created the route, if we opened our browser right now and went to `http://localhost:3000/home`, we would see an error page:

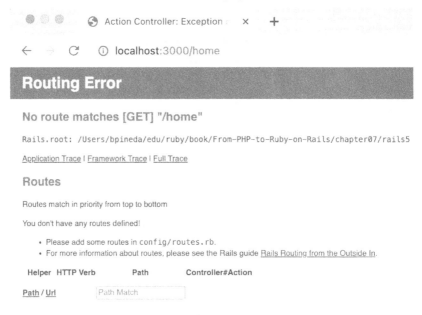

Figure 7.7 – Rails routing error page

This is because we have not defined any routes. Let's create our home route. We can do so by opening the `config/routes.rb` file:

```
Rails.application.routes.draw do
  # For details on the DSL available within this file, see http://
guides.rubyonrails.org/routing.html
end
```

So, let's define a route. Our code should now look like this:

```
Rails.application.routes.draw do
  # For details on the DSL available within this file, see
    http://guides.rubyonrails.org/routing.html
  get 'home', to: 'home#index'
end
```

Here, we are telling Rails that when the application gets a GET request with the home URL, it will point to the home controller, and execute the index action. Let's go back to our browser and refresh the page. Now, our error should be as follows:

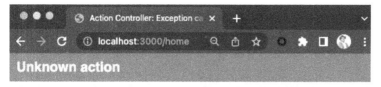

Figure 7.8 – Rails unknown action error page

So, Rails found HomeController, but it could not find the index action as it doesn't exist yet. Let's create it. Open our app/controllers/home_controller.rb file and add the following code to it:

```
class HomeController < ApplicationController
    def index
    end
end
```

This is familiar syntax – it's **object-oriented programming (OOP)** in Ruby. We have a class called HomeController that inherits from the ApplicationController class, which has a method called index. For now, this is all we are going to do for this class. Now, let's refresh our browser again; we'll see a more detailed error:

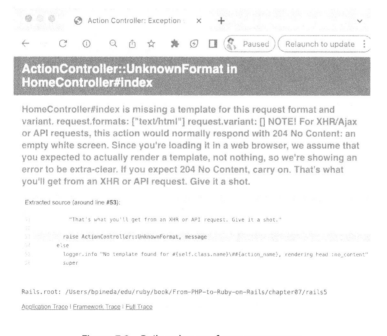

Figure 7.9 – Rails unknown format error page

This error is thrown because Rails found the controller and the `index` action but is unable to load a view into the browser because no view has been defined. Let's add the view. We can do this by creating the `app/views/home/index.html.erb` file with the following content:

```
<h2>Home controller</h2>
<h3>Index Action</h3>
```

Now, let's refresh the browser once more; we should see the following output:

Figure 7.10 – Rendered view

This is one of the features I have loved about Rails ever since I ran a Rails application for the first time. Without needing any additional configuration, Rails "knows" where to look for views. In this case, Rails "knew" that there should be a `home` folder inside the `views` folder. Rails also "knew" to look for an `index.html.erb` file within this `home` folder. In other frameworks (especially PHP ones), you must specify what file you will be rendering as a view within the controller. This becomes repetitive and impractical in the long run. Rails solves this in a very elegant and intuitive way. This is what convention over configuration refers to. Knowing the convention, we don't need to configure where Rails should look for views.

Now that we have a basic understanding of the MVC pattern and how its components make up our project structure, let's move on to the next section, where we'll learn how to use this MVC structure to send, receive, and save data with Rails.

POST, GET, and SESSION in Rails

One of the main differences while doing web development between PHP and Ruby is that PHP is web-based out of the box, while Ruby is not. All PHP needs is a web server with PHP enabled and we're good to go. For development, PHP even comes with an internal web server. On the other hand, Ruby requires the use of a framework to be able to use web protocols and tools. Ruby on Rails is not the only framework that we could use for web development, but it's the most popular one. You might also want to check out the Sinatra framework just to have another option other than Rails: `https://sinatrarb.com/`.

We will stick to Rails for web development. One of the most popular tools that's used within web development is forms. Forms help us get data from the user and handle said data to accomplish different tasks. We can set search criteria, authenticate users, or simply show previously saved data. In PHP, we can access these tools via the $_POST, $_GET, and $_SESSION arrays. In contrast, Rails handles this slightly differently but still in a useful and intuitive way. Let's start by creating some examples with values from the URL or $_GET values. First, let's add the value to the URL by adding the parameter in our browser: http://localhost:3000/home?search=php. The information in our browser will remain the same as we have not made any changes to the view. Now, let's use our index action on our Home controller and add these parameters. Once again, we must open our app/controllers/home_controller.rb file and then add the following changes:

```
class HomeController < ApplicationController
    def index
        search = params[:search]
        puts "GET value for search: #{search}"
    end
end
```

We've added a variable called search which, in turn, is using the internal params variable. params is equivalent to the $_REQUEST array in PHP. In this example, we are using it to catch the value through the URL (search) and set it to a variable. Additionally, we're showing a message with the obtained value. If we refresh our browser, we won't see any changes. Again, this is because we have not altered the view file. However, if we go to the terminal where our application is still running, we will see the following output:

```
Started GET "/home?search=php" for ::1 at 2023-07-22 11:48:18 -0700
Processing by HomeController#index as HTML
  Parameters: {"search"=>"php"}
GET value for search php
  Rendering home/index.html.erb within layouts/application
  Rendered home/index.html.erb within layouts/application (2.3ms)
Completed 200 OK in 21ms (Views: 19.3ms)
```

As we can see, the console tells us a lot about the execution. Firstly, it tells us what method (GET) we're using to call our URL. Then, it tells us the data that is being sent (search). Finally, it displays the message we added to our code. While this is not the best way to debug Rails applications, it does give us an insight as to what our code does and when it does it. In PHP, any time we write echo, it immediately passes it to the browser. In this case, should we want to pass data to the browser, first, we have to pass it to the view. So, let's do that. Let's add another line to our index action on our controller so that the code now looks like this:

```
class HomeController < ApplicationController
    def index
        search = params[:search]
```

```
        puts "GET value for search #{search}"
        @search = search
    end
end
```

This syntax looks familiar. If you don't recall, we're using an instance variable. This is the easiest way to pass values to a view. Now, let's open the view and show this `@search` value. Let's open the `app/views/home/index.html.erb` file and add code so that our view now looks like this:

```
<h2>Home controller</h2>
<h3>Index Action</h3>
<p>
    <b>Search parameter</b>: <%= @search %>
</p>
```

This also looks all too familiar. In PHP, we would use `<?= $search ?>`. In Rails, instance variables are immediately available to use on the view. Let's refresh our browser one last time; we should see the following:

Figure 7.11 – Rendered view with variables

We've successfully obtained values from the URL. Next, we'll look at values from a form sent through the `POST` method.

The `POST` method is used to send data that we don't want shown on the browser. Imagine sending a password through the browser. Anyone close by could find out our deepest secret. Fortunately, this is where `POST` values to the rescue.

First, let's add `GET` and `POST` routes to render a form and then send the form data. Let's open our routes file, `config/routes.rb`, and add the following routes:

```
Rails.application.routes.draw do
  get 'home', to: 'home#index'
```

```
  get 'user', to: 'home#user'
  post 'user', to: 'home#user'
end
```

We have to make two separate calls to `http://localhost:3000/user` – one to render the form and another one to obtain the form data. Now, let's create an action on the controller. Let's open our `app/controllers/home_controller.rb` file and add the user action:

```
class HomeController < ApplicationController
    def index
        ...
    end
    def user
        @password = params[:password]
    end
end
```

We're only passing the password to the view so that we can compare it to a value. I'd like to note here that this should not be done in a real-life scenario; we're only doing this for teaching purposes. Now, let's create a view on `app/views/home/user.html.erb` and add the form with which we'll be sending the data. For that purpose, we'll be using Rails form helpers (`https://guides.rubyonrails.org/form_helpers.html`).

Forms are easier to write with this tool, though at first, it might seem a little confusing. So, let's add the following code to our view:

```
<%= form_with url: "/user", method: :post do |form| %>
    <%= form.label :password, "Password:" %>
    <%= form.text_field :password %>
    <%= form.submit "SEND" %>
  <% end %>
```

With this code, we've created a form that calls the same URL but with the POST method. Additionally, we are sending the value of a password. If we open our browser and set our URL to `http://localhost:3000/user`, we would see the following form:

Figure 7.12 – Rendered HTML form

However, let's not send it quite yet as we haven't done anything with the value. Let's go back to the view code, `app/views/home/user.html.erb`, and add the following code so that the form looks like this:

```
<%= form_with url: "/user", method: :post do |form| %>
    <%= form.label :password, "Password:" %>
    <%= form.text_field :password %>
    <%= form.submit "SEND" %>
  <% end %>

<% if @password == '1234' %>
Password is correct
<% end %>
```

Now, let's go back to the browser and type `1234` in the password form field. Once we click on the **SEND** button, we should see the following:

Figure 7.13 – Rendered HTML form with a message

If we were to type any other value, such as `2345`, and click the **SEND** button, we would no longer see this message:

Figure 7.14 – Rendered HTML form without a message

This is because we typed in the wrong value for the password. Again, this example is only for teaching purposes. I don't think I need to tell you it's a bad idea to send a password to the view (even if you are not going to show the password), but for our purposes, I believe this example served us well. Now, let's look at session values.

Session values help save data that's unique to a browser. They can be very useful when we're dealing with a returning user or even an authentication component. For now, let's do something simple: let's try to find a session value and then create it. You already know the drill: first, we must create a route. Let's open `config/routes.rb` and add the following routes:

```
Rails.application.routes.draw do
  ...
  get 'get_name', to: 'home#name_get'
  get 'set_name', to: 'home#name_set'
end
```

Now, let's create both the `get` and `set` actions on the controller. In our `app/controllers/home_controller.rb` file, add the following:

```
class HomeController < ApplicationController
    def index
    ...
    end
    def user
    ...
    end
    def name_get
        @name = session[:name]
    end
    def name_set
        session[:name] = "David"
    end
end
```

Here, we've added the `name_get` and `name_set` actions. This is as simple as it might get on a controller. There is not much to do except set a variable called @name to pass to the view on the name_get action. In parallel, we will set the name to "David" on the name_set action. Lastly, let's add two views. First, create an `app/views/home/name_get.html.erb` file with the following content:

```
Getting the name from session <%= @name %>
```

With this, we are only displaying the value that's obtained from the session. Now, let's create the view for setting the session value. Let's create an `app/views/home/name_set.html.erb` file with the following content:

```
Setting the name for the session.
```

Once we've saved all of our changes, we can try it out in our browser. First, let's point our web browser to http://localhost:3000/get_name. This should give us the following output:

Getting the name from session

Figure 7.15 – Page with a null name

As we have not set any session values, the @name variable is empty. Now, let's open the URL in a browser that does set the http://localhost:3000/get_name value. This page should show us the following:

Setting the name for the session.

Figure 7.16 – Page for setting the session value

Now, let's open our get name URL on the browser once more (http://localhost:3000/get_name); we should now see the following output:

Getting the name from session David

Figure 7.17 – Page for getting the session value

We have successfully set up a session name and retrieved it. This is useful for visitors to our site and returning visitors who may have created an account. The correct way to go about this would be to get the username from a database, set it as a session value, and then display it to the user. Beware that sessions are based on cookies, so if a user has their cookies disabled in their browser, none of this will work. We can confirm this cookie-based behavior. If we were to open a browser in Incognito mode, our `get_name` route would display an empty name until we browsed to the `set_value` route. Just beware that just as in PHP, session values are cookie-based.

If you come from a PHP background (as I did at the time), there are a couple of additional notes that I'd like to share with you. One is that, unlike PHP, you can't have a "Ruby" web server. In the Ruby realm, your web server will always require a framework to execute Ruby code. That took me a little while to digest, but once I accepted it, Ruby on Rails became my go-to framework. The second one is more related to setting up the local environment. I tested this setup on different operating systems and different versions of Mac, Windows, and Linux with different results. I accomplished the best-unified setup by using `rbenv` (`https://github.com/rbenv/rbenv`).

This tool (`rbenv`) lets you install different versions of Ruby on your machine. One "cheat" that I found to be very useful is that when installing Rails failed with one version of Ruby, I simply tried it with another version and most of the time, the second time, Rails worked flawlessly. Try installing different versions, newer versions, and older versions, and see how they behave. Finding the subtle differences between Ruby and Ruby on Rails versions will make you a better developer.

Summary

In this chapter, we learned about Rails, the MVC application pattern, and how to install it as a gem. We also learned how to generate controllers and where these come in handy when using Rails. Lastly, we learned what developers mean when they refer to the Ruby on Rails convention over configuration "paradigm" and how this feature makes our lives easier when using Rails. Now, we are ready to start connecting and using databases with Rails Models.

8

Models, DBs, and Active Record

The **M** in the **MVC** application design pattern stands for **model**, and in this context, we will be using Ruby's model abstraction to connect to a database using another design pattern called Active Record. We must remember that while models are mostly used to connect to databases, they can also be used to connect to other data sources. We could have a model connect to a filesystem, a web service, and so on. The purpose behind a model is to organize our business rules, and that purpose may include connecting to various data sources.

In this chapter, we will first generate a model using some of our command-line generators in Rails. Then, we will use this model to connect to our database. Finally, we will look at Active Record and perform operations inside our database in a very intuitive way.

With this purpose and Active Record in mind, in this chapter, we will cover the following topics:

- Generating models using Rails
- Connecting to a database
- Active Record operations

Technical requirements

To follow along with this chapter, you will need the following:

- Any IDE to view/edit code (e.g. SublimeText, Visual Studio Code, Notepad++ Vim, Emacs, etc.)
- For macOS users, you will also need to have the Xcode command line tools installed
- Ruby version 2.6 or later installed and ready to use
- Git client installed on your local machine

The code presented in this chapter is available at `https://github.com/PacktPublishing/From-PHP-to-Ruby-on-Rails/`.

Generating models using Rails

Models are abstractions of objects we might find in everyday life. Whether they are people, books, or cars, a model serves as a representation of those objects on the database. And just like controllers, Rails comes with generators that help us create models in a very easy and intuitive way. But first, let's set up our environment. You can either start where we left off in the previous chapter, or download the example code for this chapter. If you haven't yet done so, open a terminal and type the following git command:

```
git clone https://github.com/PacktPublishing/From-PHP-to-Ruby-on-Rails.git
```

If you have already done so, then just navigate to the chapter08 folder within your project by running the following command:

```
cd From-PHP-to-Ruby-on-Rails/chapter08/rails5_models/
```

Again, let's install our dependencies with the following command:

```
bundle install
```

And to confirm our setup was done correctly, let's run the following command:

```
bundle exec rails --version
```

The output should read something like the following:

```
Rails 5.1.7
```

And now we are ready to generate our model. We will generate a model that represents people. We will add an attribute called name for each person, and another attribute called birthday. To generate our model, let's type the following command on our shell:

```
bundle exec rails generate model Person name:string birthday:date
```

With this command, we are telling our Rails generator to create a model called Person with an attribute called name, and another attribute called birthday. The name attribute will be a string, and the birthday attribute a date. Once we press the *Enter* key, we should see the following output:

```
bundle exec rails generate model Person name:string birthday:date
Running via Spring preloader in process 32161
      invoke  active_record
      create    db/migrate/20230727031200_create_people.rb
      create    app/models/person.rb
      invoke    test_unit
      create      test/models/person_test.rb
      create      test/fixtures/people.yml
```

If we look closely at this output, we should notice two important files that have been created, the migration and the model itself. Let's first open our migration file, `db/migrate/20230727031200_create_people.rb`. Its contents should look something like this:

```
class CreatePeople < Active Record::Migration[5.1]
  def change
    create_table :people do |t|
      t.string :name
      t.date :birthday
      t.timestamps
    end
  end
end
```

This file includes the instructions to generate our database structure. If we look closely, it states that it will create a `people` table with the `name`, `birthday`, and `timestamps` columns. Why was this file needed? To answer that question, we need to take a look at what Rails migrations are.

Rails migrations

In the old days, keeping track of a **database** (**DB**) was a hassle. Whenever you worked on a project with other developers that required a DB, someone had to create the DB and its tables, and often also populate it with testing data. If someone new joined the team, you would just hand them a copy of the DB and off they would go. But wait – what would happen if someone made changes to the DB structure? What if we needed a new field? What if a field was no longer needed? Then, whoever was in charge of this DB would have to make the change and then hand out the new copy of the DB to all the developers in the team. You can see how this might get out of control, especially if you have more than two developers working on the same project. In comes migrations to the rescue!

A migration is a series of commands to rebuild the structure of a DB in sequence. In the same hypothetical example that I just outlined, migrations would solve the problem with no issues. Initially, you would create a migration that created a table with certain fields. If the table required a new field, you would create another migration to create that new field. If a field was no longer required, you would create a migration to remove that field. And, as you may have noticed, the name of the migration has a timestamp. This is to run the migrations in sequence – we would first create the table, then add a field, and lastly remove a field. If a new developer joined the team, they could just run all the migrations and have the exact same database structure that everyone else has. Back to the migration at hand, we have the instructions (migration) but we still need to execute these instructions to impact the DB. So now, let's run the command to execute this migration. On the command shell, type the following command:

```
bundle exec rails db:migrate
```

This should output the following:

```
== 20230727031200 CreatePeople: migrating
======================================
-- create_table(:people)
   -> 0.0002s
== 20230727031200 CreatePeople: migrated (0.0002s)
============================
```

This means that our DB structure has been created, with a table called `people`. This is part of the Rails magic. We have not configured any DB on our project, yet if this command is successful, it means that Rails is connected to a DB. The reason behind this is that the Rails developers wanted you to have a ready-to-use project out of the box, and to do this, they made the initial project connect to a database called SQLite by default. SQLite is a series of libraries that allow us to have a ready-to-use, lightweight database based on a `sqlite3` file in your project. If you're interested in this topic, I recommend you read the SQLite official page: `https://www.sqlite.org/index.html`

We've now generated our model and we're ready to move on to the next section, where we will connect to our database using our model and the Rails configuration.

Connecting to a database

So far, we've created a `Person` model and the migrations needed for the structure of our database. Now we are ready to connect to our database. But wait, we've already connected to a database! As previously stated, if we were able to run our migration successfully, it means that we did indeed connect to the SQLite database. Now let's take a look at how Rails is configured to do this. Let's examine our Gemfile, and in doing so, we'll see the following line:

```
...
# Use sqlite3 as the database for Active Record
gem 'sqlite3'
...
```

The preceding line installs the `sqlite3` gem that allows Rails to communicate with a SQLite database. But wait, there's more. If we open the `app/config/database.yml` file, we will also see some of the database settings for our project:

```
...
default: &default
  adapter: sqlite3
  pool: <%= ENV.fetch("RAILS_MAX_THREADS") { 5 } %>
  timeout: 5000
development:
```

```
<<: *default
database: db/development.sqlite3
...
```

The `default` stanza defines the database adapter as `sqlite3` and the environment sets the database source file to be in `db/development.sqlite3`. If we check this, we'll see that the file is indeed there. The Rails migration command is the one responsible for creating this file. Don't bother opening the file as it is a binary file and unless you have a plugin to read SQLite files on your IDE, you'll only see data that only makes sense to computers and not to humans. Now let's use this newly acquired information to actually manipulate data in the database with the Rails console.

The Rails console

The creators of Rails have made an enormous effort to make Ruby on Rails the framework of choice to pair with Rails. As such, they were inspired by some of the tools that come with Ruby, and more specifically the **Interactive Ruby (IRB)** console. Rails comes with a similar console but tweaked to be able to load and query Rails components. Let's try it out with the following command:

```
Bundle exec rails console
```

This will show the following output and enable us to interact with Rails:

```
Running via Spring preloader in process 85479
Loading development environment (Rails 5.1.7)
irb(main):001:0>
```

And this is where our `Person` model comes in handy. Let's create a new object called `single_person` and add some data to our database. Inside this Rails console, let's run the following command:

```
single_person = Person.new
```

This will create an object based on the `Person` model that we defined with our `Model` file and the migrations. The previous command will output the following:

```
=> #<Person id: nil, name: nil, birthday: nil, created_at: nil,
updated_at: nil>
irb(main):002:0>
```

We can see that we've created an empty object that has no ID, no name, and no birthday. Now let's set the object's name and birthday. We'll do this by first typing the following command:

```
single_person.name = "Benjamin"
```

Our prompt will confirm with the following output that we've set the name:

```
=> "Benjamin"
```

Now let's set the birthday with the following command:

```
single_person.birthday = "1986-02-03"
```

We're setting a date in the `year-month-day` format. The preceding command sets the birth date to February 3, 1986. And just like the previous command, it will confirm this by returning the value we've just set:

```
=> "1986-02-03"
```

We can go a little further with our object and see what attributes we've set so far by just typing the name of our `single_person` variable and view the contents of the object. Let's do that as follows:

```
single_person
```

The preceding comand will return the following output:

```
=> #<Person id: nil, name: "Benjamin", birthday: "1986-02-03",
created_at: nil, updated_at: nil>
```

One thing to remember is that this information is still only available in memory. We have not persisted (or written) the data into the database. You'll hear the term *persist* often when dealing with databases, and it refers to writing the data into the database. As it stands now, if we were to leave the Rails console, the data would be lost. How do we persist the data, you may ask? Simple: we call the `save` method from our `single_person` object. But before we do that, let's confirm that there is no data in our database. We will do so by typing the following static method from our `Person` class:

```
Person.all
```

This will output the following:

```
Person Load (0.7ms)   SELECT  "people".* FROM "people" LIMIT
?  [["LIMIT", 11]]
=> #<Active Record::Relation []>
```

This output shows a command in the **Structured Query Language** (**SQL**) used by databases to manipulate data. SQL is a standard language used to "talk" to databases. Many databases use this language, so you don't have to learn a different language for each one. If you wish to know more about SQL, I recommend you take a look at this page:

```
https://aws.amazon.com/what-is/sql/
```

If you have not encountered SQL commands before, this might seem a little cryptic, but believe me, it is not so bad in reality. The first part of the output tells us Rails is loading a SQL command, the command being SELECT "people".* FROM "people". The star (*) is a filter to select all of the fields associated with the people table. In this case, it means that Rails will fetch the ID, name, birthday, and timestamp fields. The FROM part of the command tells the database engine to fetch entries from the people table without any filters. Lastly, the last line of the output tells us that there are no entries in the people table. As I mentioned before, the data is still in memory, so now let's persist the data into the database with the save method. Let's type the following command in the Rails console:

```
single_person.save
```

This will output a message confirming that we saved our data into the database:

```
irb(main):006:0> person.save
   (3.1ms)  begin transaction
  SQL (5.8ms)  INSERT INTO "people" ("name", "birthday", "created_at",
"updated_at") VALUES (?, ?, ?, ?)  [["name", "Benjamin"], ["birthday",
"1986-02-03"], ["created_at", "2023-08-06 22:11:54.475516"],
["updated_at", "2023-08-06 22:11:54.475516"]]
   (0.4ms)  commit transaction
=> true
```

Now let's again fetch all of the entries in the database with the following command:

```
Person.all
```

This will return the following output:

```
  Person Load (0.9ms)  SELECT  "people".* FROM "people" LIMIT
?  [["LIMIT", 11]]
=> #<Active Record::Relation [#<Person id: 1, name: "Benjamin",
birthday: "1986-02-03", created_at: "2023-08-06 22:11:54", updated_at:
"2023-08-06 22:11:54">]>
```

The last line states that we have indeed persisted information in the database. If we closed the Rails console and opened it up again, and fetched all the records, we would get the same result as we did just now. Congratulations, we have successfully connected to a DB using simple but powerful commands. Now it's time to take full advantage of Active Record.

Active Record operations

Active Record is a design pattern created to simplify communication with the DB. Historically, SQL is a standard for communicating with most databases. However, each database has adopted its own unique set of SQL commands and standards. While they are all very similar, each one has its own peculiarities, in part because not all databases have the same set of features. A great article detailing some of the concepts regarding the Active Record design pattern is this one:

`https://blog.savetchuk.com/overview-of-the-active-record-pattern`

As an example, PostgreSQL offers a more sophisticated set of data types than MySQL. Another example is SQLite in web applications, which is very easy to set up, but does not work well in large applications. In Rails, SQLite is mostly used for quick setups and development. Where does Active Record come into the picture? Active Record uses a technique called **Object Relational Mapper** (**ORM**). This technique involves "mapping" a database object into a programming object. An example of this mapping is where an entry on a table becomes an object, and each column becomes an attribute of said object. Why would we do this? The simple answer is that, as we are developers, it's easier to handle objects than SQL commands. The more complex answer is that Active Record uses the same language (objects) and translates these objects into any particular flavor of SQL used by a database. You could potentially switch the database type (PostgreSQL, MySQL, SQLite, etc.) with very little effort on the developer side. Actions on the database are executed using more readable commands than SQL syntax. It's much easier to learn a few intuitive commands than the whole syntax required for SQL. We've already seen this in action, but let's see the difference between a simple Active Record command and a SQL command. While still inside the Rails console, let's type the following:

```
Active Record::Base.connection.execute("Select * from people")
```

This will return an array of entries inside our database:

```
  (4.4ms)  Select * from people
=> [{"id"=>1, "name"=>"Benjamin", "birthday"=>"1986-02-03", "created_
at"=>"2023-08-06 22:11:54.475516", "updated_at"=>"2023-08-06
22:11:54.475516"}]
```

We can get the same result by using the ORM technique used by Active Record with the following command:

```
Person.all
```

The preceding command also returns an array of entries:

```
  Person Load (1.9ms)  SELECT  "people".* FROM "people" LIMIT
?  [["LIMIT", 11]]
=> #<Active Record::Relation [#<Person id: 1, name: "Benjamin",
birthday: "1986-02-03", created_at: "2023-08-06 22:11:54", updated_at:
"2023-08-06 22:11:54">]>
```

I don't know about you, but I think it's easier to remember `Person.all` than `SELECT * FROM people`. Don't get me wrong – it is always an advantage having a developer who knows SQL syntax. However, it's more advantageous to both know SQL syntax and how to exploit Active Record. Let's see other operations we can do with Active Record.

At this point, I believe it would be very useful to install a client to analyze our SQLite data visually. There are many clients and browser plugins for this task, but I recommend DB Browser for SQLite. You can check out its page here:

`https://sqlitebrowser.org/`

This will accomplish the goal of visualizing data on Windows and Mac, and even some distributions of Linux, but for those platforms for which this tool is not available, you can also rely on Chrome's SQLite Manager for Google Chrome plugin:

`https://chrome.google.com/webstore/detail/sqlite-manager-for-google/aejlocbcokogiclkcfddhfnpajhejmeb`

They all work in a similar manner, and besides, we just want to use the tool as a visual data browser.

Once we've installed the tool, let's open the database file. In this case, the DB file is in `chapter08/rails5_models/db/development.sqlite3`. With the DB Browser for SQLite app open, let's click on the **Open Database** button shown here:

Figure 8.1 – Open Database button in DB Browser for SQLite

Then let's navigate into our `development.sqlite3` file:

Figure 8.2 – Navigating into the sqlite3 file

Once we open that file, we will be able to view the tables that we've created so far, along with a few others that Rails creates on its own.

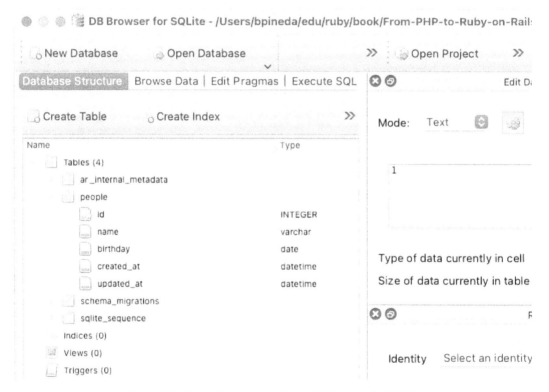

Figure 8.3 – Open the people table on DB Browser for SQLite

We can ignore all the other tables for now, and just focus on the `people` table. As you can see, we have the same columns (`id`, `name`, `birthday`, `created_at`, and `updated_at`) as we saw on the `Person` object when we created an instance of the `Person` model. But more than the structure, we're interested in the entries (or records) inside this table. Let's right-click on the `people` table and let's select the **Browse Table** option, as shown in the following screenshot:

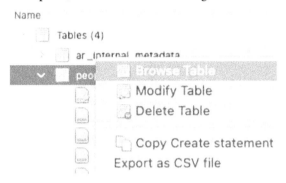

Figure 8.4 – Browse table data on DB Browser for SQLite

Now we should see the single entry that we added when playing around with the Rails console:

id	name	birthday	created_at	
	Filter	Filter	Filter	Filter
1	1	Benjamin	1986-02-03	2023-08-06 22:11:54.475516	2023-

Figure 8.5 – Entries on the people table shown on DB Browser for SQLite

The entry should have the same data that we fed to the Rails console.

We've confirmed the initial data was set correctly, but now it's time to use Active Record to create new records on the database.

Creating records

We previously saw that we could add entries to our database by creating a `Person` object, adding attributes (`name` and `birthday`), and finally saving the record. But there is a one-liner that does the same thing. Let's try the following line inside our Rails console:

```
Person.create(name: "Oscarr", birthday: "1981-02-19")
```

It should output the following:

```
    (2.7ms)  begin transaction
  SQL (7.6ms)  INSERT INTO "people" ("name", "birthday", "created_at",
"updated_at") VALUES (?, ?, ?, ?)  [["name", "Oscarr"], ["birthday",
"1980-02-19"], ["created_at", "2023-08-07 01:14:35.044370"],
["updated_at", "2023-08-07 01:14:35.044370"]]
    (0.5ms)  commit transaction
=> #<Person id: 2, name: "Oscarr", birthday: "1981-02-19", created_at:
"2023-08-07 01:14:35", updated_at: "2023-08-07 01:14:35">
```

The value for the name "Oscarr" is on purpose. As we can see, the create method generates a SQL statement to create a record on the same table we've been working on but with different attributes. The more attributes we have, the more lines of code we would need had we used the other method to add data. Both ways are valid ways to insert data into our database. I just wanted to demonstrate both options so that you can choose the one that is more convenient for your specific use case. Now, let's confirm that this new entry does in fact exist on the database. Let's go back to the DB Browser for SQLite app, and refresh the view either with the refresh button or by pressing *CMD + R* for Mac users or *Ctrl + R* for Windows and Linux users. This should now show the new entry on the table:

Figure 8.6 – New entries on the people table shown on DB Browser for SQLite

Oh, but wait. We've made two mistakes. I made typo by adding the name "Oscarr" when I meant to type just "Oscar". I also made a mistake with the year, as I meant to add 1980 instead of 1981. This fortunate mistake brings us to the next operation: SELECT.

Selecting record(s)

So far, we've seen one method to select all of our entries: the all method. But Active Record comes with two other very useful methods: first and last . As the name implies, we can select the first record of any selection. Let's do that by typing the following command on the Rails console:

```
Person.all.first
```

This should return the following output:

```
   Person Load (0.9ms)   SELECT   "people".* FROM "people" ORDER BY
"people"."id" ASC LIMIT ?   [["LIMIT", 1]]
=> #<Person id: 1, name: "Benjamin", birthday: "1986-02-03", created_
at: "2023-08-06 22:11:54", updated_at: "2023-08-07 02:20:36">
```

As you can see, the command selects the very first entry from our `people` table. Now let's try the `last` method by typing the following on the Rails console:

```
Person.all.last
```

This should output the following:

```
   Person Load (1.8ms)   SELECT   "people".* FROM "people" ORDER BY
"people"."id" DESC LIMIT ?   [["LIMIT", 1]]
=> #<Person id: 2, name: "Oscarr", birthday: "1981-02-19", created_at:
"2023-08-07 01:14:35", updated_at: "2023-08-07 02:24:21">
```

We've selected the last record on our database. These methods come in handy when looking for test data. Now let's use the `where` method to filter data by a determined field. Let's try the following code on the Rails console:

```
Person.where( name: "Benjamin" )
```

This will output the following:

```
   Person Load (0.9ms)   SELECT   "people".* FROM "people" WHERE
"people"."name" = ? LIMIT ?   [["name", "Benjamin"], ["LIMIT", 11]]
=> #<Active Record::Relation [#<Person id: 1, name: "Benjamin",
birthday: "1986-02-03", created_at: "2023-08-06 22:11:54", updated_at:
"2023-08-07 02:20:36">]>
```

This code has selected all entries that have the name `"Benjamin"`. In this case, there is just one entry. However, there is a little catch here that we should be careful with. Notice that after the word `Relation` in the previous output, there is a square bracket (`[`), which is eventually closed almost at the end of the line (`>]>`). This is because when we use the `where` method, it always returns an array of objects. This is useful when displaying data on a grid or table on the view, but can be tricky when we want to select a single entry. Now, let's talk about selecting single records. Before updating any record, we need to select which record we're going to modify. For that purpose, the implementation of Active Record on Rails comes with two handy methods. The first one is `find_by`. The `find_by` method requires a parameter in the form of a hash that includes the attribute that we want to filter, followed by the value. In this case, we want to filter by the `name` attribute and the `Oscarr` value. Let's test this by typing the following on the Rails console:

```
found_person = Person.find_by name:"Oscarr"
```

This will return the following output:

```
irb(main):002:0> found_person = Person.find_by name:"Oscarr"
  Person Load (0.8ms)  SELECT  "people".* FROM "people" WHERE
"people"."name" = ? LIMIT ?  [["name", "Oscarr"], ["LIMIT", 1]]
=> #<Person id: 2, name: "Oscarr", birthday: "1981-02-19", created_at:
"2023-08-07 01:14:35", updated_at: "2023-08-07 01:14:35">
```

Rails returns the first entry that it finds with the criteria that we supplied to the `find_by` method. In this case, it finds the first entry that complies with having the name equal to `"Oscarr"`. We can confirm this by typing any attribute and viewing its contents. Let's try this by typing the following line in the Rails console:

```
found_person.id
```

And this will return the following output:

```
2
```

We can do the same with any other attribute. Let's try it with the `birthday` attribute. Let's type the following on our Rails console:

```
found_person.birthday
```

And we should get the following output:

```
Thu, 19 Feb 1981
```

So, as you can see, the `found_person` object has the entry that we were looking for. However, this comes with a caveat. There may be more than one person with the same name. If we were looking to select the second person, then our code would fail as the `find_by` method automatically returns the first found entry. To solve this conundrum, Active Record provides a special method called `find`. This method assumes that our table has an `id` column, which is unique for each entry. So, in our previous use case, if there were two people with the same name, we would just filter it by the unique ID. In this case, we would just type the following in our Rails console:

```
found_person = Person.find(2)
```

And this would output the same as before:

```
irb(main):015:0> Person.find(2)
  Person Load (4.6ms)  SELECT  "people".* FROM "people" WHERE
"people"."id" = ? LIMIT ?  [["id", 2], ["LIMIT", 1]]
=> #<Person id: 2, name: "Oscarr", birthday: "1981-02-19", created_at:
"2023-08-07 01:14:35", updated_at: "2023-08-07 01:14:35">
```

Should there be another entry with the same name, it wouldn't matter to us. Our code would select the one with the `id` equal to 2. Now that we've selected an entry, let's move on to updating its contents.

Updating records

Just like creating records, there are a couple of ways that we can update a record in the database. Since we've already selected our record that has a typo in the name, let's see the first option we can use to update records. Let's say we typed the following code into our Rails console:

```
found_person
```

This would output the following record:

```
=> #<Person id: 2, name: "Oscarr", birthday: "1981-02-19", created_at:
"2023-08-07 01:14:35", updated_at: "2023-08-07 01:14:35">
```

With this, we can confirm that this is the right record we want to modify. To modify the name, we would type the following code on our Rails console:

```
found_person.name = "Oscar"
```

This would just output the string we have just assigned to our `name` attribute:

```
=> "Oscar"
```

But remember what we said about the object: this change is still only in memory. We need to persist the change. We would use the same `save` method as before. Let's type the following on the Rails console:

```
found_person.save
```

This would output the following:

```
irb(main):019:0> found_person.save
   (0.3ms)  begin transaction
  SQL (0.4ms)  UPDATE "people" SET "name" = ?, "updated_at" = ? WHERE
"people"."id" = ?  [["name", "Oscar"], ["updated_at", "2023-08-07
02:14:06.188761"], ["id", 2]]
   (0.9ms)  commit transaction
=> true
```

This will save our change into the database and return a true value. This true value will come in handy later on in the next chapter. But for now, we can just confirm this change by opening DB Browser for SQLite and refreshing the view. It should now show the correct name:

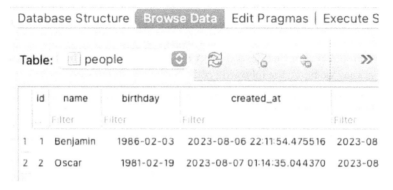

Figure 8.7 – Modified entry on the people table as shown in DB Browser for SQLite

That was one way to modify a record. However, there is another way using the `update` method. Let's try it with the following code on the Rails console:

```
found_person.update(birthday: "1980-02-19")
```

This would output the following:

```
   (0.4ms)  begin transaction
  SQL (0.4ms)  UPDATE "people" SET "birthday" = ?, "updated_at" = ?
WHERE "people"."id" = ?  [["birthday", "1980-02-19"], ["updated_at",
"2023-08-07 02:24:21.753388"], ["id", 2]]
   (0.7ms)  commit transaction
=> true
```

Now let's confirm the change again on the DB Browser for SQLite app. Let's just refresh the view and we should see the change show up:

Figure 8.8 – Updated entry on the people table as shown in DB Browser for SQLite

So as you can see, we've updated our record in two different ways. Again, both of these methods are valid and you can choose whichever method fits your needs more. Now let's look at the last method (for now), which is the `destroy` method.

Deleting record(s)

So far, we've created, selected, and updated records in our database. The last Active Record action we're going to look at is the destroy action. You should be especially careful with this action as this deletes data from your database without any confirmation required beforehand. Furthermore, this action is permanent – once the destroy action has been done, it cannot be reverted. So, let's first create another entry with the following command on the Rails console:

```
Person.create( name: "Bernard", birthday: "1981-07-16" )
```

This should output the following:

```
   (0.5ms)  begin transaction
  SQL (1.0ms)  INSERT INTO "people" ("name", "birthday", "created_at",
"updated_at") VALUES (?, ?, ?, ?)  [["name", "Bernard"], ["birthday",
"1981-07-16"], ["created_at", "2023-08-07 02:37:29.615141"],
["updated_at", "2023-08-07 02:37:29.615141"]]
   (0.4ms)  commit transaction
=> #<Person id: 3, name: "Bernard", birthday: "1981-07-16", created_
at: "2023-08-07 02:37:29", updated_at: "2023-08-07 02:37:29">
```

And once again, let's refresh our view on the DB Browser for SQLite app:

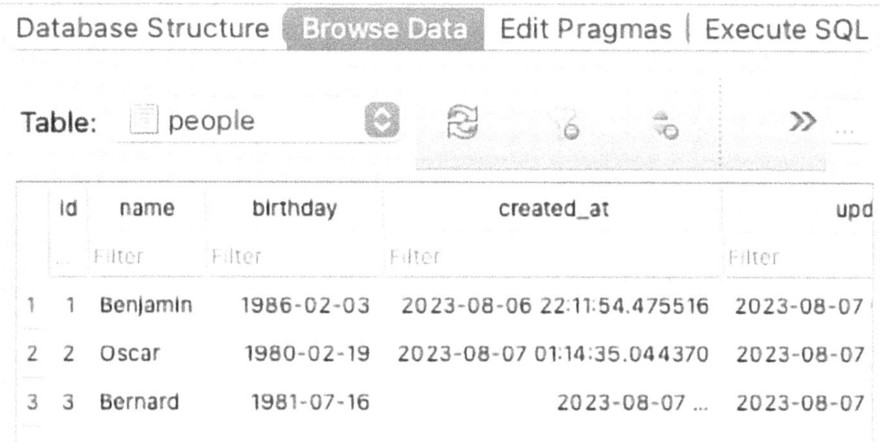

Figure 8.9 – New entry on the people table as shown in DB Browser for SQLite

Now that we've confirmed that the new entry exists, we can proceed to delete it. Just like the `update` method, we first must select an entry on the database. Let's do this by typing the following on the Rails console:

```
person_to_delete = Person.find(3)
```

This should output the following:

```
  Person Load (0.4ms)  SELECT  "people".* FROM "people" WHERE
"people"."id" = ? LIMIT ?  [["id", 3], ["LIMIT", 1]]
=> #<Person id: 3, name: "Bernard", birthday: "1981-07-16", created_
at: "2023-08-07 02:39:56", updated_at: "2023-08-07 02:39:56">
```

With this, we confirm that we've selected the right record. Finally, let's delete the record with the following code on our Rails console:

```
person_to_delete.destroy
```

This would output the following:

```
   (0.5ms)  begin transaction
  SQL (0.5ms)  DELETE FROM "people" WHERE "people"."id" = ?  [["id",
3]]
   (0.9ms)  commit transaction
=> #<Person id: 3, name: "Bernard", birthday: "1981-07-16", created_
at: "2023-08-07 02:39:56", updated_at: "2023-08-07 02:39:56">
```

As you can see, it generated and executed the code to delete the entry. If we go to our DB Browser for SQLite app and refresh the view, we should see that the entry no longer exists:

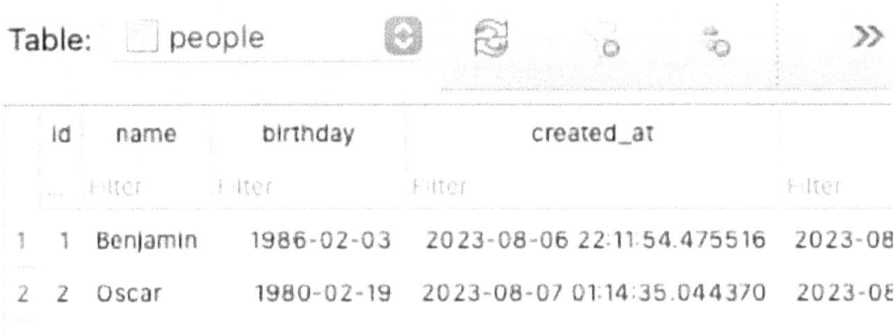

	Id	name	birthday	created_at	
		Filter	Filter	Filter	Filter
1	1	Benjamin	1986-02-03	2023-08-06 22:11:54.475516	2023-08
2	2	Oscar	1980-02-19	2023-08-07 01:14:35.044370	2023-08

Figure 8.10 – Deleted entry on the people table as shown in DB Browser for SQLite

As we can see, the entry has been deleted and is forever gone. I cannot stress enough how dangerous this operation can be when developing an application. All I can say is, be careful while using it.

You may have noticed that all the data manipulation on the database was done through the Rails console. This is because I believe the Rails console is the easiest way to understand and learn how to use Active Record actions. Once we have mastered these easy-to-use intuitive methods, then applying this knowledge in our controllers and views can be achieved without any difficulty whatsoever. Should you wish to learn more about these Active Record actions, please take a look at the Active Record basics page:

```
https://guides.rubyonrails.org/active_record_basics.html
```

Summary

In this chapter, we learned about models, migrations, and the Rails console as the go-to tool to easily manipulate data on a database. We also learned how useful the implementation of Active Record is on Rails and how we can communicate with a database with very easy-to-use commands. Now we are ready to put it all together by fetching data from a database and displaying it on the view, which is what we'll be doing in the next chapter.

9

Bringing It All Together

So far, we have seen how to use controllers, views, and models in a somewhat detached manner. In the previous chapter (*Models, Databases, and Active Record*), we manipulated data on our database. However, we didn't see how to interact with the database data from our controller, much less how to load that database data into our view. In this chapter, we are going to see how everything comes together – that is, we'll load a model from the controller and pass the model data to our view so that the end user will see data on the browser. We will also do the reverse, which is getting data from the user into our database, starting from the view and ending on the model. Furthermore, we will also learn the Rails way to perform these actions, as they are quite different from the way we would do these tasks in PHP.

With models, views, and controllers in mind, in this chapter, we will cover the following topics:

- Setting up our initial application with generators
- Processing data the Rails way
- Do not, I repeat, do not reinvent the wheel

Technical requirements

To follow along this chapter, we will need the following:

- Any IDE to view/edit code (e.g., SublimeText, Visual Studio Code, Notepad++ Vim, Emacs, etc.)
- For macOS users, you will also need to have Xcode Command Line Tools installed
- Ruby version 3.1.1 or later installed and ready to use
- A Git client installed on your local machine

The code presented in this chapter is available at `https://github.com/PacktPublishing/From-PHP-to-Ruby-on-Rails/`.

Project preparation

Prior to setting up our application, we are going to do some additional configuration, depending on the operating system. We will separate the configuration into two sections – Windows configuration and Linux-based systems (including macOS).

Windows configuration

In *Chapter 7*, we configured our Windows environment to use **rbenv** to be able to use Ruby 2.6.10. If you haven't done so, please go back to the *Installing Ruby on Rails in Windows* section, as this is required for this chapter. For Rails 7 (which we will install in this chapter), we will require Ruby 3.1.1 installed and some dependencies that aren't easily available for Windows. We will use the Git SDK's bash shell (which we also installed in *Chapter 7*) to solve this issue. So, let's open a Windows PowerShell and type the following command:

```
C:\git-sdk-64\git-bash.exe
```

This will open a Git Bash console, which looks and behaves a lot like a Linux shell. Let's confirm that we have Ruby available by typing the following command:

```
ruby –version
```

This should output the following:

```
ruby 3.1.3p185 (2022-11-24 revision 1a6b16756e) [x64-mingw32]
```

If you're not familiar with this version of Ruby, it's because it comes with the Git SDK. Now, let's install bundler for Ruby 3.1.3 with the following command:

```
gem install bundler
```

Next, let's update our system's bundler with the following command:

```
gem update –system 3.3.3
```

Now, we are ready to set up our application.

Linux-based system configuration

For macOS and Linux-based systems (Ubuntu and Debian), we're going to depend on rbenv to install Ruby 3.1.1. If you haven't installed rbenv, please refer to *Chapter 7* to view the instructionson on how to install rbenv on Linux. With rbenv available, let's install another version of Ruby with the following command on a shell:

```
rbenv install 3.1.1
```

Now that Ruby 3.1.1 has been installed, let's set the default Ruby to Ruby 3.1.1 with the following command:

```
rbenv global 3.1.1
```

Let's confirm that the correct Ruby version has been activated by running the following command:

```
ruby --version
```

This should output the following:

```
ruby 3.1.1p18 (2022-02-18 revision 53f5fc4236) [x86_64-linux]
```

We should install bundler for this version of Ruby with the following command:

```
gem install bundler
```

Now, we're ready for our next Rails project.

Setting up our application

For this exercise, we will have a hypothetical scenario in which we are Thomas A. Anderson, and we work for a respectable software company. We will play the part of a junior web developer in terms of our knowledge of Rails, and we will be assigned a simple task. The client has requested a simple address book structure where they can save their friends' contact information – name, last name, email, and phone number. So, let's get to work. Make sure you have Ruby version 3.1.1 or above installed, or we might encounter issues with the project. We could download a template application that we already have or clone it from GitHub. In case you haven't done so, open a terminal and type the following `git` command:

```
git clone https://github.com/PacktPublishing/From-PHP-to-Ruby-on-
Rails.git
```

If you've already done so, just navigate into the `chapter09/rails7_original` folder inside our project with the following command:

```
cd From-PHP-to-Ruby-on-Rails/chapter09/rails7_original/
```

For this small project, the client requested that we use Rails 7, as it's the version they have used in other projects. It also gives us a chance to see Rails 7 in action. Now, let's install our project dependencies with the following command:

```
bundle install
```

To confirm our setup was done correctly, let's run the following command:

```
bundle exec rails --version
```

The output should read something like this:

```
Rails 7.0.6
```

And this is where our work as a Rails developer starts. We're going to use some Rails magic to generate most of our code. Let's generate a `friends` controller with all the methods that we are going to be calling – `index`, `new`, `edit`, `update`, `destroy`, and `create`. Let's go to our shell and run the following command:

```
bundle exec rails generate controller Friends index new edit update
destroy create
```

This should generate the following output:

```
create    app/controllers/friends_controller.rb
 route    get 'friends/index'
          get 'friends/new'
          get 'friends/edit'
          get 'friends/update'
          get 'friends/destroy'
          get 'friends/create'
invoke    erb
create      app/views/friends
create      app/views/friends/index.html.erb
create      app/views/friends/new.html.erb
create      app/views/friends/edit.html.erb
create      app/views/friends/update.html.erb
create      app/views/friends/destroy.html.erb
create      app/views/friends/create.html.erb
...
```

Coming from the PHP world, and more specifically, Laravel, you may find the previous command slightly familiar. In Laravel, you'd generate an equivalent controller with the following command:

```
php artisan make:controller FriendsController --resource
```

They both generate similar functionality (the `friends` controller) and the `--resource` option at the end generates the correct HTTP verbs. In Rails, the `generator` command we just ran takes as its first argument the controller name (Friends) and the rest as controller methods. The command is also very verbose regarding what it actually generates. It not only created our controller but also a view for each of the methods we passed to the command. We can see this by opening the `app/views/friends/` folder.

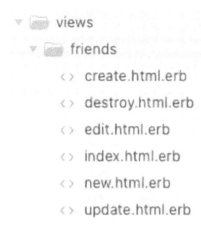

Figure 9.1 – Generated views for the Friends controller

Additionally, the controller generator modified our `routes.rb` file, which defines all the URLs for our actions inside the controller. If we open `config/routes.rb`, we see our newly created routes:

```
Rails.application.routes.draw do
  get 'friends/index'
  get 'friends/new'
  get 'friends/edit'
  get 'friends/update'
  get 'friends/destroy'
  get 'friends/create'
  # root "articles#index"
end
```

While this is fine and dandy, we can also do it the Rails way. Let's delete all the routes and just leave two lines inside the `do` block, so our `routes.rb` file now looks like this:

```
Rails.application.routes.draw do
  resources :friends
  root "friends#index"
end
```

This looks a lot cleaner, though slightly cryptic, as we don't know (yet) what this resource call does. The resource call generates RESTful routes for the following actions – `index`, `new`, `edit`, `create`, `update`, and `destroy`. This simply means that all these actions should be called using the correct HTTP verbs – GET, POST, PATCH, PUT, and DELETE. I don't want to overwhelm you with too much information here, so to simplify this, we'll just say we need some parameters through the URL, and some others to be "hidden" from the user. If you're curious about RESTful and its uses, please take a look at the following links:

- `https://guides.rubyonrails.org/routing.html`
- `https://www.redhat.com/en/topics/api/what-is-a-rest-api`
- `https://aws.amazon.com/what-is/restful-api/`
- `https://www.ibm.com/topics/rest-apis`

Now, to the next step. Let's generate a model that will represent our "friends" in the database. We'll generate our model with the following command on the shell:

```
bundle exec rails generate model Friend first_name:string last_
name:string email:string phone:string
```

This will generate the following output:

```
invoke  active_record
create    db/migrate/20230817022418_create_friends.rb
create    app/models/friend.rb
invoke    test_unit
create      test/models/friend_test.rb
create      test/fixtures/friends.yml
```

The model generator created the migration to create a `friends` table. The table will have the `first_name`, `last_name`, `email`, and `phone` fields. From what we learned in the previous chapter, we know that we must run the migration to effectively generate our database structure. We'll do that by running the following command on our shell:

```
bundle exec rails db:migrate
```

If this is not new to you, it might be because other PHP frameworks have similar tools. For Laravel, we would execute the following command:

```
php artisan migrate
```

For Symfony, we would write the following command:

```
bin/console doctrine:migrations:migrate
```

For CodeIgniter, we would write the following command:

```
spark migrate
```

We can infer from these examples in PHP frameworks that the migration tool has been in the web framework market for a while, and it's here to stay.

The last step to our setup is going to be something we didn't cover in the previous chapter, and it is related to Rails models. As an additional help for developers to get a working environment as soon as possible, Rails integrated a tool called database seeds. Seeds allow us to generate test data based on our model structure. I confess I cheated a little bit by providing you with an already-working seed file. It's in the db/seeds.rb file. Let's look at one record in that file:

```
...
Friend.create(first_name: "rasmus", last_name: "lerdorf", email:
"rasmus@email.com", phone: "+1(669)1111111")
...
```

This piece of code is pretty self-explanatory. It creates a `Friend` entry with the first name (`rasmus`), the last name (`lerdorf`), the email address (`rasmus@email.com`), and a phone number (`+1(669)1111111`). Of course, this is all fake data, but it will be useful for us whenever we start using the database. The last step is to run this seed and add these records to our database. We do this with the following command on our shell:

```
bundle exec rails db:seed
```

This command will generate the five records we find in the seeds file. This was all the setup we needed for our initial application. Now, it's time to manage this data.

Processing data

Up until this point, we've manually modified data within the database. By manually, I mean all inside the Rails console. However, as our project requirement is to let the users handle the `friends` entries, we will do so by integrating our model with our controller and our view so that a user can see the `friends` entries in a friendly interface. We will be creating a **CRUD** interface. Yes, it sounds ugly, but it's the acronym software engineers came up with. It stands for **CReate Update Delete**, which is exactly what we are going to build – an interface to create, update, and delete records.

Setting up the CRUD interface

The first step is to confirm that the data is, in fact, in our database. From our previous chapter, we know that we can call the Rails console for this, so let's do that by running the following command:

```
bundle exec rails console
```

This should change our shell to look like this:

```
Loading development environment (Rails 7.0.6)
irb(main):001:0>
```

Now, let's type the following command on this console:

```
Friend.all
```

This will show all of the friends entries on the database. It should show something like this:

```
    Friend Load (0.4ms)  SELECT "friends".* FROM "friends"
=>
[#<Friend:0x00000001067cbe90
  id: 1,
  first_name: "rasmus",
  last_name: "lerdorf",
  email: "rasmus@email.com",
  phone: "+1(669)1111111",
  created_at: Thu, 17 Aug 2023 02:41:30.679843000 UTC +00:00,
  updated_at: Thu, 17 Aug 2023 02:41:30.679843000 UTC +00:00>,
 ...
 #<Friend:0x00000001068232f8
  id: 5,
  first_name: "david heinemeier",
  last_name: "hansson",
  email: "my5@email.com",
  phone: "+1(918)5555555",
  created_at: Thu, 17 Aug 2023 02:41:30.687162000 UTC +00:00,
  updated_at: Thu, 17 Aug 2023 02:41:30.687162000 UTC +00:00>]
irb(main):002:0>
```

The content has been truncated for brevity, but you should see five records that correspond to what's on the seed file. This output confirms that the data is in the database. Now, let's exit the Rails console by typing the following on the shell:

```
exit
```

Now, let's start our Rails application with the following command:

```
bundle exec rails server
```

This command should output the following:

```
=> Booting Puma
=> Rails 7.0.6 application starting in development
```

```
=> Run `bin/rails server --help` for more startup options
Puma starting in single mode...
* Puma version: 5.6.6 (ruby 3.1.1-p18) ("Birdie's Version")
*   Min threads: 5
*   Max threads: 5
*   Environment: development
*          PID: 14464
* Listening on http://127.0.0.1:3000
* Listening on http://[::1]:3000
Use Ctrl-C to stop
```

Lastly, open the browser of your choice and go to `http://127.0.0.1:3000/any`. This should show the following Rails error page:

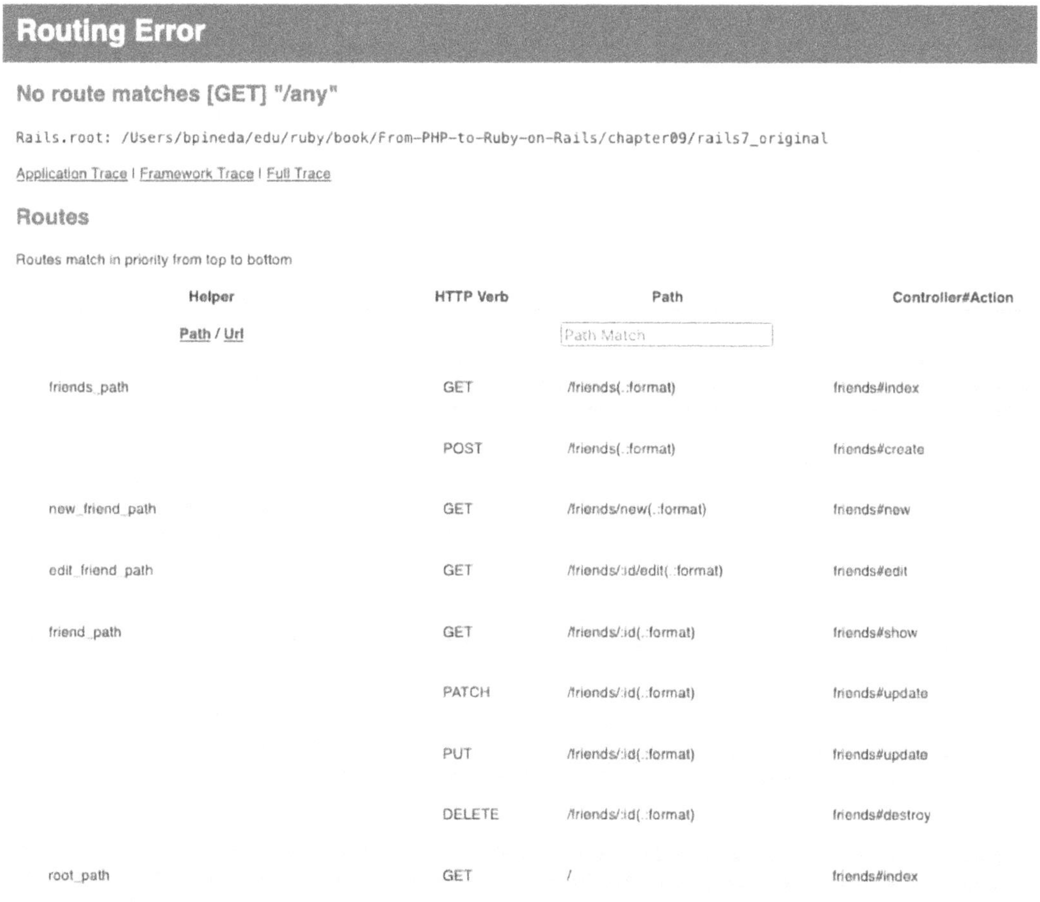

Routing Error

No route matches [GET] "/any"

Rails.root: /Users/bpineda/edu/ruby/book/From-PHP-to-Ruby-on-Rails/chapter09/rails7_original

Application Trace | Framework Trace | Full Trace

Routes

Routes match in priority from top to bottom

Helper	HTTP Verb	Path	Controller#Action
Path / Url		Path Match	
friends_path	GET	/friends(.:format)	friends#index
	POST	/friends(.:format)	friends#create
new_friend_path	GET	/friends/new(.:format)	friends#new
edit_friend_path	GET	/friends/:id/edit(.:format)	friends#edit
friend_path	GET	/friends/:id(.:format)	friends#show
	PATCH	/friends/:id(.:format)	friends#update
	PUT	/friends/:id(.:format)	friends#update
	DELETE	/friends/:id(.:format)	friends#destroy
root_path	GET	/	friends#index

Figure 9.2 – The Rails Routing Error page

I purposely mentioned opening a non-existing route to view this page. Whenever you open a route that is not registered on the `routes.rb` file, Rails shows this error page, which shows us all the defined routes for our application. As I mentioned earlier, the resource call generated a lot of routes for us that are related to our `friends` component. We'll start with `root_path`. Let's find the `root_path` entry on this error page. Once we find the entry, we can see that it corresponds to our application's root URL (`/`), and whenever we go to this route on the browser, we execute the `index` method that is inside the `friends` controller, as shown in the last column (`friends#index`). This error page is basically a map of URL addresses and what action on the controller they will execute. From this page, we learned that we are going to need to modify the `index` method on our `friends` controller file in `app/controllers/friends_controller.rb`. We should see the following code inside this file:

```
class FriendsController < ApplicationController
  def index
  end
  def new
  end
  def edit
  end
  def update
  end
  def destroy
  end
  def create
  end
end
```

Note that all these actions were generated by the controller generator, so we don't start from scratch. Also, these are all the actions that we'll build to create our CRUD interface.

Listing data

Let's focus on the `index` method. We want to show all our records on the `index` method, so we will now load the `Friend` model and select all of our entries in the database. With these changes in mind, the `index` method should now look like this:

```
class FriendsController < ApplicationController
  def index
    @friends = Friend.all
  end
  ...
```

By adding the @ symbol in front of our `friends` variable, we set the variable to be an instance variable. The way Rails works is that this instance variable is then passed to the view. Note that this is not the only way to pass data from the controller to the view, but it is a very simple way to do it. Now, let's go back to the browser but change the URL to `http://127.0.0.1:9000/`. We should see the following screen:

Friends#index

Find me in app/views/friends/index.html.erb

Figure 9.3 – The Rails index page

But wait! The data that we loaded is not being shown. This is because while we do have Rails magic, we don't have Rails miracles. We still have to work on the view. So, let's open the `app/views/friends/index.html.erb` view and add the data that we just fetched from the database, with the `Friend` model. Our view currently looks like this:

```
<h1>Friends#index</h1>
<p>Find me in app/views/friends/index.html.erb</p>
```

Let's remove that code and add a table and a cycle to iterate inside the `@friends` variable. Our code in the view should now look like this:

```
<% @friends.each do |friend| %>
  <%= friend.first_name %></br>
<% end %>
```

With this code, for every friend entry on the database (`@friends.each do |friend|`), we will rename each entry `friend`. Note the code tags (`<% %>`) on the first line of code. They are very much like the PHP tags we use to embed PHP code in a page (`<?php ?>`), and just like the PHP tags, anything inside these tags will be processed as Ruby code. Since the code is simply a cycle to fetch every DB entry, any code after line one will be repeated for every entry in the database until the Ruby cycle is closed on line three. On line two, we use a different set of tags (`<%= %>`). These tags will not only process whatever is inside them as Ruby code, but they will also output the result to the browser. They are exactly like the PHP tags (`<?= ?>`). It's sort of like an `echo` statement but on the browser. Now, let's refresh the browser, which should show a page like this:

Figure 9.4 – The Rails index page with data

Wow! We've done it. We've loaded data from the database to the controller and then to the view. I don't know about you, but the first time I saw this I was really excited, not only because of the result but also because I understood what I was doing with the framework. I hope you do too now. Unfortunately, this was just a test to make sure our data was being loaded correctly into the view. A proper grid will have titles and more fields. Let's remove the code we just added to the view and add the following code:

```
<table border=1>
  <tr>
      <th>FIRST NAME</th>
      <th>LAST NAME</th>
      <th>ACTION</th>
  </tr>
  <% @friends.each do |friend| %>
    <tr>
      <td><%= friend.first_name %></td>
      <td><%= friend.last_name %></td>
      <td><a href="/friends/<%= friend.id %>/edit">
        DETAILS</a></td>
    </tr>
  <% end %>
</table>
```

With this change, the first six lines of code build a table and the title rows. On line seven, we create the cycle to iterate between each database entry. Inside the cycle, we show the first and the last name. Lastly, we've added a link to the edit action. This is to work on our next view. If we refresh the browser, we should see the following page:

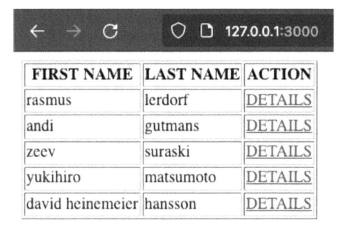

Figure 9.5 – A Rails index table with data

Now, let's work on the update page of our CRUD web interface.

Updating data

To edit an entry, we first must select that entry. If we take a closer look at *Figure 9.2*, we can see that the edit_friend_path route passes a parameter (:id). Unlike classic PHP, we do not explicitly pass parameters by the URL. Instead, we embed them inside the URL so that our route would be http://localhost:3000/friends/2/edit instead of http://localhost:3000/friends?id=2. In Rails, we seldom use explicit URL parameters (?parameter_name=value). With that in mind, as we already have the name of the parameter, we can use it to select a single entry. Let's open our edit method on the friends controller in app/controllers/friends_controller.rb. The method is currently empty. It should look like this:

```
class FriendsController < ApplicationController
...
  def edit
  end
...
```

Now, let's use our model to select a single user by its ID. Our code will now look like this:

```
class FriendsController < ApplicationController
...
  def edit
    @friend = Friend.find(params[:id])
  end
...
```

Now that we've selected the entry, let's see some more Rails magic in action. Let's open the edit view on `app/views/friends/edit.html.erb`. This should look like this:

```
<h1>Friends#edit</h1>
<p>Find me in app/views/friends/edit.html.erb</p>
```

Now, let's delete the preceding HTML code and replace it with the following code:

```
<%= form_with model: @friend do |form| %>
  <%= form.label :first_name %><br>
  <%= form.text_field :first_name %><br>

  <%= form.label :last_name %><br>
  <%= form.text_field :last_name %><br>

  <%= form.label :email %><br>
  <%= form.text_field :email %><br>

  <%= form.label :phone %><br>
  <%= form.text_field :phone %><br>

  <%= form.submit %>
<% end %>
```

Rails comes with another set of tools for tasks we do over and over. These tools are called *helpers*. Helpers are functions that we can call to generate a task for us. There are many types of helpers, but for now, we'll use form helpers that assist us in building forms for data processing.

If you're interested in learning more on this topic of form helpers, please refer to the Ruby guides:

`https://guides.rubyonrails.org/form_helpers.html`

In the preceding code, we chose the `form_with` helper to generate a form to update the `Friend` entry. Then, inside the form, for each field that we have on the database (`first_name`, `last_name`, `email`, and `phone`), we generated a label and a field. Lastly, we added a submit button to send the data back to the controller for processing. Now, let's open our browser and click on the first DETAILS link on the index page. This will take us to the `http://127.0.0.1:3000/friends/1/edit` URL, and it should show the following page:

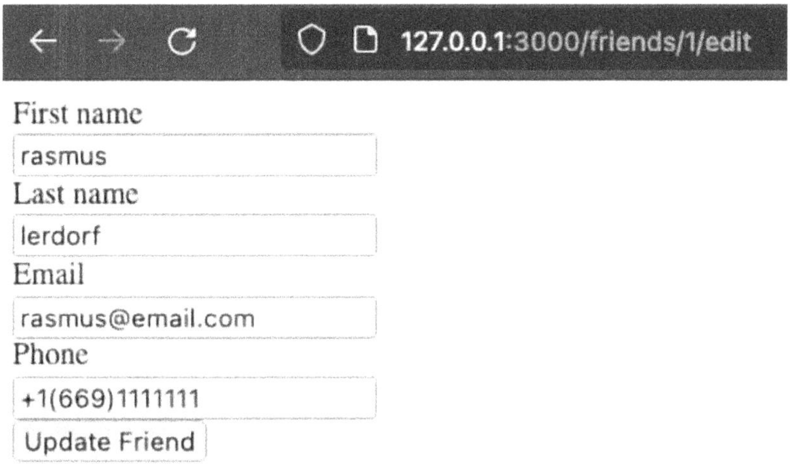

Figure 9.6 – A Rails edit form with data

And voilà! With very little code, we've generated a form that shows the current field values and lets us modify these values. However, we're still missing the code to modify any of these values on the database. So, let's go back to the controller on app/controllers/friends_controller. rb, but now, we'll add a method to help us process the form.

Creating data

Our last method (create) is at the end of our class:

```
class FriendsController < ApplicationController
...
  def create
  end
end
```

Let's add a private method called friend_params right after our create method. Our code should look like this:

```
class FriendsController < ApplicationController
...
  def create
  end

  private
  def friend_params
    params.require(:friend).permit( :first_name,
      :last_name, :email, :phone )
```

```
      end

   end
```

With this method, when called, we let Rails know that the data sent through a form should have a friend index, and inside this index, it may have the first_name field, last_name field, and so on. In PHP terms, this would be equivalent to sending data in the following array:

```
   $_REQUEST['friend'] = array("first_name"=>"rasmus",…);
```

I'm oversimplifying this process, but in essence, the method requires and allows certain parameters.

If you wish to learn more about parameters, do take a look at these pages:

- https://apidock.com/rails/ActionController/Parameters/require
- https://apidock.com/rails/ActionController/Parameters/permit

For now, let's implement this friend_params method. Do keep in mind that to show the edit form, the method we call is edit, but to modify the data on the database, we'll call the update method. Currently, the update method is empty. Let's modify the method so that it will now look like this:

```
   …
   def update
     @friend = Friend.find(params[:id])
     if @friend.update(friend_params)
       redirect_to friends_path
     end
   end
   …
```

With the @friend variable, we again select the record that we are going to modify. Once this record is selected, we call the update method on this object, which is where the update on the database will happen. Lastly, we'll use the redirect_to helper to send the user to the friends page on the browser. This code is very concise and almost reads like sentences – *find friend* and *if friend is updated with friend parameters, redirect to friends path*. This is Ruby at its finest. The only thing we haven't analyzed from this snippet of code is the friends_path helper. However, it's simple. We'll refer again to *Figure 9.2*, in which we see a table with all of our defined routes. As we find the friends_path helper on this page, we can determine that when we use that alias, we can send a user to the correct controller and method (friends#index).

Now, let's move on to creating a new `friend` entry. As with the edit page, let's first generate our new entry page. In the `app/controllers/friends_controller.rb` file, let's modify the empty `new` method. It should now look like this:

```
...
def new
  @friend = Friend.new
end
...
```

As we are going to use the `form_for` helper, we need to pass an empty model object for the helper to be able to generate the form correctly. Let's open the `new` view in `app/views/friends/new.html.erb`, which currently looks like this:

```
<h1>Friends#new</h1>
<p>Find me in app/views/friends/new.html.erb</p>
```

Let's delete the preceding content and replace it with the following code:

```
<%= form_with model: @friend do |form| %>
  <%= form.label :first_name %><br>
  <%= form.text_field :first_name %><br>
  <%= form.label :last_name %><br>
  <%= form.text_field :last_name %><br>
  <%= form.label :email %><br>
  <%= form.text_field :email %><br>
  <%= form.label :phone %><br>
  <%= form.text_field :phone %><br>
  <%= form.submit %>
<% end %>
```

You might have noticed that this is the exact same view as the edit page. Most of the time, we should not repeat the exact same code, but since we are still learning Rails, we get a pass here. Now, let's go back to the controller in `app/controllers/friends_controller.rb` and modify the `create` method. It's empty, but we should add some code so that it looks like this:

```
...
def create
  if Friend.create( friend_params )
    redirect_to friends_path
  end
end
...
```

Just like the update method, we call the create method with the friend params to create a new entry. Once the entry is created, we redirect the user to the friends index page. Now, let's try it out on the browser. On the browser, open the http://127.0.0.1:3000/friends/new URL, which should show the same form as the edit page, but without any data:

Figure 9.7 – The Rails new entry form

Let's fill the fields with new data, as shown here:

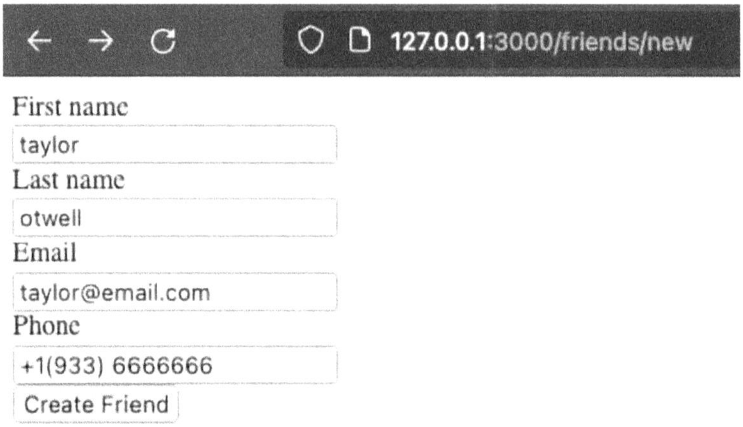

Figure 9.8 – The Rails new entry form with data

When we click on the **Create Friend** button, a new entry is added to the database, and we are redirected to the `friends` index page, which should show the newly created friend:

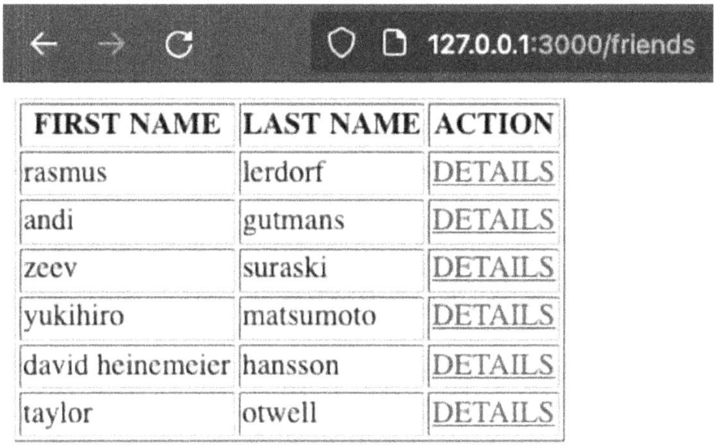

FIRST NAME	LAST NAME	ACTION
rasmus	lerdorf	DETAILS
andi	gutmans	DETAILS
zeev	suraski	DETAILS
yukihiro	matsumoto	DETAILS
david heinemeier	hansson	DETAILS
taylor	otwell	DETAILS

Figure 9.9 – The Rails index page with a new entry

OK, we are almost there – just a few more lines of code. The only method left to cover is the `destroy` method, but it's as easy as the other methods we've coded so far.

Deleting data

Let's open up our edit view on `app/views/friends/edit.html.erb` and add another form at the end of the file. Our form at the end of the file should look like this:

```
...
<%= form_with model: @friend, method: :delete do |form| %>
  <%= form.submit "DELETE" %>
<% end %>
```

Beware of not modifying any of the code that was already in this `edit.html.erb` view at the beginning of the file. We should add the preceding code at the *end* of the file. This new form generates a delete button. Note how we are passing an additional parameter, `method:`, with the value of the `:delete` symbol. This will automatically make the form send the data to the appropriate `destroy` method. Now, let's work on the `destroy` method on the controller in `app/controllers/friends_controller.rb`. As with the other methods we've covered so far, this method should be empty. Let's add the following code to it:

```
...
def destroy
  @friend = Friend.find(params[:id])
  @friend.destroy
```

```
    redirect_to friends_path
end
...
```

With this ominously looking code, we're telling Rails to select a user by their ID, delete the record from the database, and finally, redirect the user to the `friends` index page. Now, let's give it a try on the browser. Let's open our browser and go to the `friends` index page: `http://127.0.0.1:3000/friends`. Click on the last link at the bottom, which should open the edit page that corresponds to Taylor Otwell:

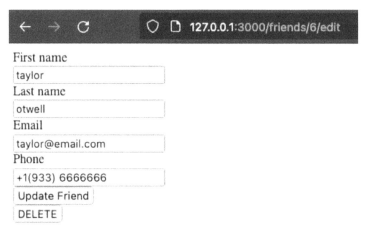

Figure 9.10 – A Rails edit page with the latest entry

Note how we now have a **DELETE** button. Let's click on it, and just as quickly as we created this entry, we now have deleted it. The table should now look like this (without the Taylor Otwell record):

FIRST NAME	LAST NAME	ACTION
rasmus	lerdorf	DETAILS
andi	gutmans	DETAILS
zeev	suraski	DETAILS
yukihiro	matsumoto	DETAILS
david heinemeier	hansson	DETAILS

Figure 9.11 – A Rails friends index page with one less entry

And with that, my dear reader, we have successfully created our CRUD interface for our friend address book. We can now list the existing friends, create new ones, modify the existing ones, and lastly, delete any records we no longer need. Just so we don't get confused as to what our controller in `app/controllers/friends_controller.rb` should look like at the end of this exercise, let me share the whole file again with all the changes we've made so far:

```ruby
class FriendsController < ApplicationController
  def index
    @friends = Friend.all
  end

  def new
    @friend = Friend.new
  end

  def edit
    @friend = Friend.find(params[:id])
  end

  def update
    @friend = Friend.find(params[:id])
    if @friend.update(friend_params)
      redirect_to friends_path
    end
  end

  def destroy
    @friend = Friend.find(params[:id])
    @friend.destroy
    redirect_to friends_path
  end

  def create
    if Friend.create(friend_params)
      redirect_to friends_path
    end
  end

  private
  def friend_params
    params.require(:friend).permit( :first_name, :last_name, :email,
:phone )
  end
end
```

While our application can now handle records, it still has room for improvement, such as the following:

- We could use a navigation bar or at least a link to the "new" page

- We should refactor the form views so that we use the same form to modify and add records

- We should use validations

- We should show errors if any of the actions fail

I tried to over-simplify many of these concepts to focus more on a pragmatic approach. However, if you are interested in a more detailed set of examples, there are always the guides from Ruby on Rails: `https://guides.rubyonrails.org/getting_started.html`.

The examples in the preceding web page will cover a far more detailed version of what we saw in this chapter. You could make everyone proud and take on these improvements on your own.

Back to the task at hand – the hypothetical client accepted our simplified version of the CRUD interface. However, someone asked about security. They don't want just anyone to be able to see their friend entries on the app. They want to at least protect the application with a login page. If you were thinking that we need to program this authentication component, think no more, as we have just the tool for this.

Do not, I repeat, do not repeat yourself

If you've worked with frameworks in the past, you may be familiar with the **Don't Repeat Yourself (DRY)** principle, even though the principle is more focused on coding and coding style. If you're not, or just need a reminder, the DRY principle simply states that you should not repeat yourself.

You can find out more details here:

`https://docs.getdbt.com/terms/dry`

As much as we possibly can, we should try not to repeat our code. As an example in this application, we repeated the code on the `edit` and `new` views. Using the DRY principle, we should refactor our code so that it uses the same form for both actions. In the same manner, instead of building everything on your own and from scratch, you should reuse functions, tools, and even libraries altogether. One task that we as developers have done over and over is to authenticate users. If you have an authentication code that works, you may have even copied it from a previous project. However, an open source tool can improve your code. One advantage of using an open source tool to handle your authentication is that it's tested against many more scenarios than you could have ever imagined on your own. Another reason to use an open source tool is that it may be ready to use and simple to incorporate into our project. There are several gems for user authentication, but for now, we'll use one that is very easy to use called Devise: `https://github.com/heartcombo/devise`.

Devise is a gem that, interestingly enough, generates several Rails components that we can use for our application. Devise will generate views, routes, and helpers to assist us with our user authentication. So, let's incorporate a new gem into our application. The first step is going to be to stop the Rails application server. Open the shell where the application is currently running and press the *Ctrl* key and *C*. This should stop the Rails application and return the shell to normal. The next step is to include the Devise gem in our Gemfile. Let's open our `./Gemfile` file at the root of our project (`chapter09/rails7_original/Gemfile`), and add the following code right after the Rails gem line. The Gemfile should now look like this:

```
...
gem "rails", "~> 7.0.6"

gem "devise"
...
```

Now, let's install our gem. Let's go to our shell and run the following command:

```
bundle install
```

The command should output a message related to the devise gem:

```
...
Using responders 3.1.0
Using importmap-rails 1.2.1
Fetching devise 4.9.2
Using rails 7.0.6
Installing devise 4.9.2
Bundle complete! 11 Gemfile dependencies, 64 gems now installed.
Use `bundle info [gemname]` to see where a bundled gem is installed.
Post-install message from devise:
...
```

Our gem has been installed, but it still needs to run additional tasks, and we still need to add some configuration to our app in order for us to be able to use Devise. Let's run the `install` command on our shell:

```
bundle exec rails generate devise:install
```

The outcome of this installation is a set of instructions that we must do before being able to use the gem in our project:

```
      create  config/initializers/devise.rb
      create  config/locales/devise.en.yml
===============================================================
```

```
Depending on your application's configuration some manual setup may be
required:

  1. Ensure you have defined default url options in your environments
files. Here is an example of default_url_options appropriate for a
development environment in config/environments/development.rb:
        config.action_mailer.default_url_options = { host: 'localhost',
port: 3000 }

     In production, :host should be set to the actual host of your
application.

     * Required for all applications. *

  2. Ensure you have defined root_url to *something* in your config/
routes.rb.
      For example:

      root to: "home#index"

     * Not required for API-only Applications *

  3. Ensure you have flash messages in app/views/layouts/application.
html.erb.
      For example:

      <p class="notice"><%= notice %></p>
      <p class="alert"><%= alert %></p>

     * Not required for API-only Applications *

  4. You can copy Devise views (for customization) to your app by
  ...
```

We must follow these post installation instructions for the gem to work properly. The first task refers to adding a line of configuration to our environment config file. Let's do that. Let's open `config/environment/development.rb` and add the following line to it. Our `config` file should now look like this:

```
...
# Don't care if the mailer can't send.
  Config.action_mailer.raise_delivery_errors = false
  config.action_mailer.perform_caching = false
  config.action_mailer.default_url_options = { host: 'localhost',
port: 3000 }
```

We've added a line to set the `config.action_mailer.default_url_options` flag after the `config.action_mailer.perform_caching` flag is set. In a production setting, the configuration line we just added would enable password recovery through email. As this will not work locally, we can ignore it, but the config still needs to be set in place for Devise to work. The second instruction refers to having a root route. We can also ignore this instruction, as our application already includes a root route. The third task requires that we modify our application layout to include an HTML placeholder for errors and messages. So, let's do just that. Let's open the `app/views/layouts/application.html.erb` file. This file controls how our application will look. Anytime you need to make a view change on a general level, this is the place to go. Let's add those placeholders so that our application layout now looks like this:

```
...
<body>
  <p class="notice" ><%= notice %></p>
  <p class="alert"><%= alert %></p>
  <%= yield %>
</body>
...
```

Whenever Devise alerts any messages regarding the login process, these placeholders will now show those messages (if any are present). From post installation instructions to get the devise gem to work correctly, we are at the last task (number 4) and this task can be ignored, as it refers to customizing our login views. We're almost ready to use Devise, but as I mentioned before, this gem will need a database model to save our user data. So, let's run the following command on our shell to do so:

```
bundle exec rails generate devise User
```

This should output the following:

```
invoke  active_record
create    db/migrate/20230817200425_devise_create_users.rb
create    app/models/user.rb
invoke    test_unit
create      test/models/user_test.rb
create      test/fixtures/users.yml
insert    app/models/user.rb
 route  devise_for :users
```

From analyzing this output, we can see that both a user model and a database migration have been created. This command also added the login routes to our application. Remember what we do after we create a database migration? We need to run the database migration so that the user structure is added to the database. Let's do just that. Run the following command:

```
bundle exec rails db:migrate
```

This will output the changes made to the database:

```
== 20230817200425 DeviseCreateUsers: migrating ===================
-- create_table(:users)
   -> 0.0015s
-- add_index(:users, :email, {:unique=>true})
   -> 0.0004s
-- add_index(:users, :reset_password_token, {:unique=>true})
   -> 0.0003s
== 20230817200425 DeviseCreateUsers: migrated (0.0023s) ===========
```

Our gem is now ready to be used by our application. For now, let's limit all access to our application so that no method on the controller can be viewed without signing in. The beginning of our app/ controllers/friends_controller.rb file should now look like this:

```
class FriendsController < ApplicationController
  before_action :authenticate_user!
  Def index
  ...
```

By adding the second line of code, the before_action helper will perform the user authentication prior to executing any other action on the controller. Now, it's time to try it out. Let's go to our shell and start the Rails application server with the following command:

```
bundle exec rails s
```

Once our application is up and running, we should go back to the browser and open http://127.0.0.1:3000/, and you will be asked for an email address and a password:

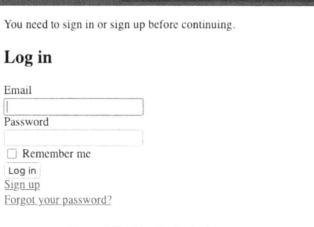

Figure 9.12 – The Devise login page

If you see this form, it means that the Devise gem is working. If you try to view any page (e.g., `http://127.0.0.1:3000/friends/1/edit` or any other existing route), you should be redirected to the login page. There are two ways to create users with the Devise gem in place. We can use our Rails console, or we can just sign up. Let's use the sign-up method. Click on the **Sign up** link, and it should take you to the **Sign up** form:

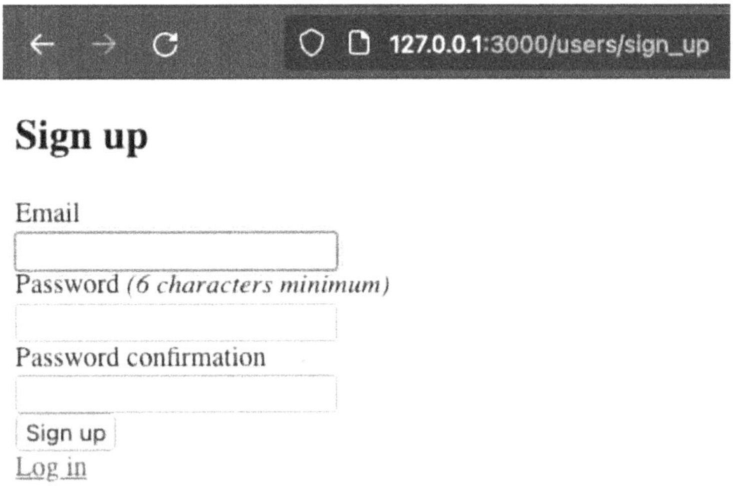

Figure 9.13 – The Devise sign up page

Let's add an email address, `admin@email.com`, and `123456` as the password. Then, when you click on the **Sign up** button, you should immediately see the page you were trying to browse before being redirected. As the last page I tried to browse was the edit page, I am now shown that. However, you can also browse the index page at `http://127.0.0.1:3000/` – try it. You should be able to see the index page again:

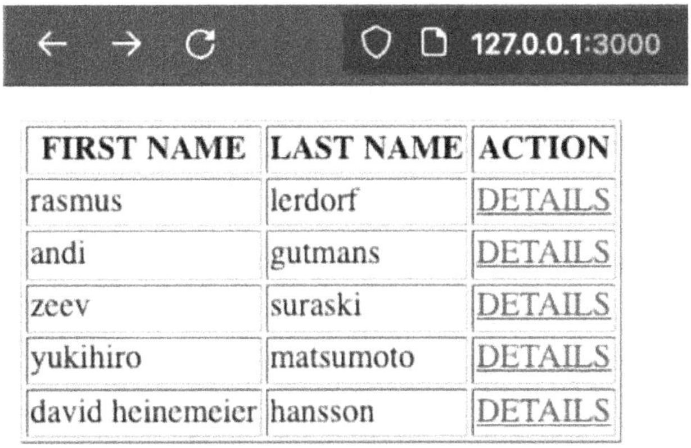

FIRST NAME	LAST NAME	ACTION
rasmus	lerdorf	DETAILS
andi	gutmans	DETAILS
zeev	suraski	DETAILS
yukihiro	matsumoto	DETAILS
david heinemeier	hansson	DETAILS

Figure 9.14 – The authenticated index page

As our pièce de resistance, let's add a logout link, but only to our index page. Open the `app/views/friends/index.html.erb` file, and add this code to the end of the file:

```
...
<%= form_with model: @user, url: destroy_user_session_path, method:
:delete do |form| %>
  <%= form.submit "Sign out" %>
<% end %>
```

Now, the form looks fairly familiar. Devise uses the same `form_with` helper to build a form to log out with. Let's go back to our browser and refresh the index view. It will look like this:

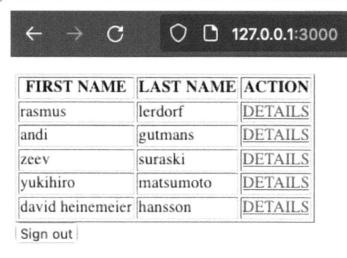

Figure 9.15 – The index page with a Sign out button

We now have a **Sign out** button. If we click it, our session ends, and we are redirected to the login page again. We can log in again using the credentials we created a few steps back.

Congratulations! Our work here is done. As always, there is room for improvement and further learning. This gem is super handy and has helped me solve the authentication piece of an application many times. One thing (among so many) that you may have noticed is that even though this gem uses session values to handle the authentication, you never see these session values, and you never handle them directly. That is the Rails way of doing things. We always tend to hide the session layer of an application with helpers. Devise comes with some helpers that will help you within your code to show or hide components, depending on your authentication status. You may want to check the `user_signed_in?`, `current_user`, and `user_session` helpers on the Devise documentation page. Additionally, you can add several other customizations that you may want to add to your authentication mechanism. Be sure to play around with the gem, and learn on your own what other configurations might be useful to you.

Summary

Wow! We covered a lot of ground in this chapter. We learned how to load data from a model to a controller to finally show data on the view. We also learned how to interact with forms and impact the database with the MVC architecture of Rails. Last but not least, we learned how to integrate the Devise gem with our application to leverage our authentication mechanism, instead of building one from scratch.

Now, we are ready for our last chapter, where we'll explore some additional information regarding hosting our Rails application on a server.

10

Considerations for Hosting Rails Applications versus PHP Applications

Congratulations for making it to this point. You've created a simple Rails application that uses controllers, views, and models. You used generators to prep for your development. You also set up the database with migrations. Lastly, you included a gem to help you out with authentication. And now, you're happy to say, this application works on your machine. Now it's time to share your application with the world (or maybe just a client), and herein lies an important difference between a PHP application and a Rails application: the hosting.

In this chapter, we are going to go through certain aspects of hosting that we must consider when releasing our Rails application. We'll compare different hosting options, as well as examine additional concepts we need for Rails applications. Then, we will look at how the Rails framework behaves depending on the environment setup. More specifically, we'll look at error reporting on production environments.

With Rails hosting in mind, in this chapter, we will cover the following topics:

- PHP versus Rails in terms of price
- Do it yourself, or have it done for you?
- Why nginx?
- Error gossip

Technical requirements

To follow along this chapter, you will need the following:

- Any IDE to view/edit code (e.g., SublimeText, Visual Studio Code, Notepad++, Vim, Emacs, etc.)

- For macOS users, you will also need to have the Xcode command line tools installed

- Ruby version 3.1.1 or later installed and ready to use

- Git client installed on our local machine

The code presented in this chapter is available at `https://github.com/PacktPublishing/From-PHP-to-Ruby-on-Rails/`.

PHP versus Rails in terms of price

Before you give me grief about this unfair comparison, I'm not comparing PHP and Rails directly. They can't really be compared, as one is a programming language and the other a framework. A more fair comparison would be comparing the Laravel framework with the Rails framework. What I'm trying to convey is a PHP universe in which many tools live. But to do that, we must go back in time for a bit to when PHP finally became object oriented. This object-oriented PHP opened up a whole new world of possibilities. In 2004, PHP was already popular, and with this new feature (object-oriented programming), it became even more popular. WordPress became the standard for managing blogs and eventually websites. More web frameworks developed with PHP came into the picture: CodeIgniter, Symfony, Laravel, just to name a few. Joomla and Drupal gave developers yet another option that was a mix of a framework and a **Content Management System** (**CMS**). Thanks to this popularity, everyone was offering hosting options that supported PHP, and very cheaply if I may add. As other technologies became available, hosting for these technologies was also available but at a much higher cost. With the risk of sounding outrageous, I will say that I had a running application for a client in a server that cost them just 20 USD each year. Suffice it to say, in 2023, things have become a little more balanced than in 2004, but you can still find very cheap options for PHP applications, while (for the most part) Rails hosting will be slightly more costly. A quick search will land us with several options for Rails hosting, including the following more popular ones:

- DigitalOcean (`https://www.digitalocean.com/`)

- Amazon Lightsail (`https://aws.amazon.com/lightsail/`)

- Heroku (`https://www.heroku.com/platform`)

- AWS (`https://aws.amazon.com/`)

- Google Cloud (`https://cloud.google.com/`)

- Azure (`https://azure.microsoft.com/`)

In terms of cost, Amazon Lightsail is probably the most cost-effective option you will find (at the time of this writing) with plans for as little as 3.50 USD a month. This option offers a simple-to-use environment with **Amazon Web Services** (**AWS**) behind the scenes, but without the complexity. DigitalOcean offers a great option in terms of price and flexibility starting at 6 USD a month with a virtual machine that they fondly call a Droplet. This plan includes a PostgreSQL database. Heroku is a little more pricey, starting from 5 USD, and does not include a database in that price. A small database will add an additional 7 USD each month for a total of 12 USD. The last two options I'd say are only for more advanced needs and perhaps more advanced clients. They can be cheap (initially), but the more you need, the more expensive they become. Also, setting everything up in any cloud service (be it AWS, Google Cloud, or Azure) can be a real challenge as you need to fully understand elements of the cloud ecosystem, as opposed to other options that deliver a ready-to-use interface for your application.

Additionally, depending on what your application does, the cost will vary and you won't really know how much you'll be charged until the end of the month. They do have built-in cost calculators and give more-or-less precise monthly estimates, but since they charge for everything (execution time of your virtual machine, networking, data transfer, disk usage, fixed IPs, and many other things), the costs will vary from month to month. You have absolute control of how your application is deployed and executed, but it comes at a cost. And then there are the worst-case scenarios, where if your security is compromised, an attacker might take control of not only your server but also your infrastructure, potentially costing you thousands of dollars for a simple mistake. That's not to say that you shouldn't consider the cloud options as viable. They're just not an option for beginners or even intermediate developers. They're enterprise solutions for those companies that can handle the risk and benefit from their usage. Let's take a closer look at these differences between the bundled solutions (DigitalOcean, Amazon Lightsail, and Heroku) and the build-your-own options (AWS, Google Cloud, and Azure).

DIY or have it done for you

We've seen, in terms of costs, the different options that are available to us for hosting our application. However, this isn't the only distinguishing factor to consider while determining and implementing a solution. They also differ in terms of philosophy and usage. For now, we'll stick to one option that is bundled, packaged, and ready to be used. By *bundled solution*, I'm referring to a solution that gives you a server that is installed, configured, and ready to use. For simplicity, I picked DigitalOcean and deployed our small application, but rest assured that the other bundled options will be very similar in implementation. As this incurs a cost, I won't add the steps to follow along, so you just can sit back and enjoy the ride. You can typically select an optimized server image from a marketplace. Most bundled solutions have their own marketplaces where you can search and select an image (or template) that suits your needs. In our case, we can go to `https://marketplace.digitalocean.com/` and review the available options. Of course, they will have the classic **Linux-Apache-MySQL-PHP** (**LAMP**) images ready to go, but we're interested in the Ruby-on-Rails counterpart, which we can easily find here:

```
https://marketplace.digitalocean.com/apps/ruby-on-rails
```

Once we select the technology we will use, we can view what this virtual machine (or Droplet) includes:

Software Included ⟨?⟩

Package	Version	License
Ruby	3.2.0	2-clause BSD License
Rails	7.0.4.2	MIT
Puma	6.0.2	Custom
Postgres	12.4	Postgres SQL
Nginx	1.17.10	Custom
Node.js	12.19.0	Custom
Certbot	0.40.0	Apache 2

Figure 10.1 – Rails virtual machine

The greatest advantage of acquiring a bundled solution is that you don't have to worry about installing Ruby, the Rails gem, and any other dependencies that we might need for our application. As we can see in *Figure 10.1*, this virtual machine will have Rails 7.0.4.2 and all the dependencies needed for our application to work. Now, we're presented with access to a shell where we can either log in or transfer our application files onto this server. It even comes with an example application already configured so that we know for a fact that Rails is installed and ready to be used. When I browsed to the IP that DigitalOcean provided for me, I encountered this familiar page:

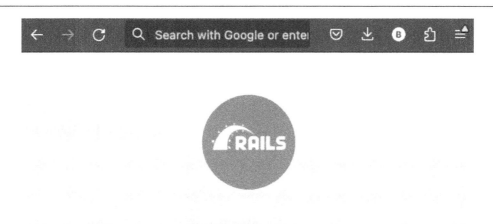

Rails version: 7.0.6
Ruby version: ruby 3.2.0 (2022-12-25 revision a528908271) [x86_64-linux]

Figure 10.2 – Rails example application on DigitalOcean

Deploying our application was simple enough, only requiring the same steps we did locally:

1. Copy the source code to the server.

2. Run Rails migrations.

3. Run Rails seeds.

4. Add a use

    And voilà:

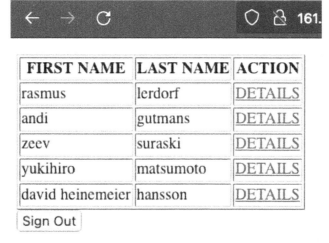

FIRST NAME	LAST NAME	ACTION
rasmus	lerdorf	DETAILS
andi	gutmans	DETAILS
zeev	suraski	DETAILS
yukihiro	matsumoto	DETAILS
david heinemeier	hansson	DETAILS

Sign Out

Figure 10.3 – Deployed Rails application on DigitalOcean

The same application we had locally has now been deployed to a hosting solution. With a few differences here and there, I can guarantee you that the other bundled options (such as Heroku or Amazon Lightsail) will provide a similar environment to get our app running. The automation of this process (the deployment) is outside of the scope of this book, but if you're interested in more complex options for deployment, I suggest you take a look at Jenkins, Docker, and **Continuous Integration/Continuous Delivery (CI/CD)**:

- `https://www.jenkins.io/`
- `https://www.docker.com/`
- `https://docs.docker.com/samples/rails/`
- `https://www.synopsys.com/glossary/what-is-cicd.html`

For simplicity with our application, we chose the use of a SQLite database. It's easy to install and implement locally, but for a real-world scenario, we would go for a more robust option such as MySQL or PostgreSQL. This Droplet additionally comes with a ready-to-use PostgreSQL database. This is what any bundled option would provide for us.

To recap, these are the advantages of the bundled option:

- Can be set up in no time
- Environment ready to use
- Dependencies resolved
- Robust database ready

However, this solution may not be a perfect fit for everyone. Most bundled solutions are flexible in terms of Ruby, but not in terms of the operating system. These solution providers can and will delete deprecated packages. Some solution providers even update packages (for security purposes) without your permission and may impact the behavior of your application. Additionally, when you need to customize your server, that may be your cue to consider the non-bundled solution options.

DIY

In contrast to the bundled options for hosting, the do-it-yourself options give you much more flexibility. Why would we need that flexibility? There are many cases where this is necessary, but one specific use case I can think of for this scenario is to scale up an application's resources. Let's say, for example, that your application is initially set up to serve 500 users, but you notice that you now have a database with 10,000 users. Your application is now very slow, but increasing the size (memory and CPU) of your server for 10,000 users would be way too expensive. You also notice that the number of concurrent users (i.e., users using the application at the same time) reaches 4,000 and not 10,000. In comes auto-scaling to the rescue!

Auto-scaling determines the resource requirements at a given moment and automatically scales up as concurrent users peak, and then scales back down when user concurrency drops. By *scaling up* I'm referring to the platform creating more servers on the fly to be able to handle more users. As the hosting service only charges you when those additional servers are actually running, the whole process can save the company money as you don't have a whole army of servers turned on the whole time, but only when the number of users peaks. Additionally, your application's availability increases with this approach. I'm oversimplifying this whole process, but I do hope you get where I'm going with this. This is only one of many scenarios where a non-bundled solution would be the best fit. If you are interested in learning more about the topic of auto-scaling, I recommend you look at the official AWS page for auto-scaling:

```
https://aws.amazon.com/autoscaling/
```

I'm going to choose AWS for our hypothetical solution, but it would be implemented similarly on any other cloud. To deploy our simple application on AWS, we would create an EC2 instance and add the security groups.

Once we launch our instance, we would wait for it to come up, which might take a couple of minutes. Once our instance was ready, we would access it through SSH and then begin our Ruby configuration. This would include installing Ruby, the bundler, GCC compilers – the works. Once Ruby was ready, we would install our Rails gem. Then we would upload our application code to our virtual machine and run the initial setup (installing dependencies, Rails migrations, Rails seed, and user setup). Then we'd start the server. This is where things would start to get more and more complicated. We would have a number of options for making this application available to the world. One option would be to open port 3000 to the world, and away we go. However, the Rails server should never be exposed directly to the outside world. We'll see why that is in the next section, but for now, let's just stick to that principle. We'll need to set up Nginx as our web server and have it redirect calls to our Rails app. Once this was ready, we would be good to go.

As you can see, this seems more complicated than the bundled option. With this simple example, there isn't any easily discernable advantage to building it on our own, and that's because it doesn't really give us any advantage. At least, not for our specific case – firstly, because AWS will always be an expensive choice, and secondly, because it is an enterprise solution, and as such, as in most enterprise solutions, the configuration and deployment will be more complex, albeit resulting in many more choices for your application. While I wouldn't recommend deploying our application in any DIY public cloud (AWS, Google Cloud, or Azure) to share it with the world, I would recommend you do this as an exercise as it will get you familiar with the operations of cloud solutions. Nowadays, familiarity with this type of technology is a must for developers.

While we don't really need to go into the details of these solutions (at least not for now), I believe we do need to get a grasp of certain concepts regarding our application deployment. Deploying our application behind a web server (Nginx) is one of these concepts, which we will look at in more depth in the next section.

Why nginx?

Coming from a PHP background, one of the concepts that was difficult for me to grasp was Rails' lack of the out-of-the-box server functionality seen in PHP. With PHP, if it is installed, you can open a shell and type the following:

```
php -S localhost:9000
```

This will bring up an internal PHP server. You can now open a browser, point it to `http://localhost:9000/`, and that's all you need to do. Any PHP scripts we add to the same folder where we started the PHP server will be available to said server. We don't need any PHP framework to start programming in PHP. We can use this internal server for development and once we deploy our PHP application to a production server, our application just requires a web server that has PHP enabled. This is an oversimplification of how it's actually done, but in essence, that's all that's needed for PHP servers.

In the good ol' days, Apache was the way to go. These days, you can still use Apache, but Nginx has gained a lot of ground here, to the point that Nginx is nowadays almost (if not) the standard. What is Nginx? Nginx (according to its website) is an advanced load balancer, web server, and reverse proxy designed to handle high-traffic websites and applications. It is widely used as a web server and has reportedly been adopted by Netflix and Airbnb, among others. With these names involved, we can safely assume its efficiency whilst handling web-related components is extremely high. Why should we use Nginx as a web server for Rails? The answer is delegation. A web server should handle things such as static assets (images, stylesheets, etc.), file uploads, SSL certificate display, and some DDoS protection, to name just a few. Rails (and many other web frameworks) are very capable of handling most of these tasks too, but why reinvent the wheel when we can have our Rails application only needing to worry about Rails tasks, and Nginx worrying about the web-related tasks? Additionally, Nginx is much faster and more efficient at handling these tasks than any web framework. As a matter of fact, our demo bundled hosting solution (DigitalOcean) comes with Nginx installed and configured to point to the example Rails application. I disabled the Rails upstream and set the Nginx page to the default, and this is what I got:

Figure 10.3 – Nginx default page on DigitalOcean

The task of setting up the Nginx configuration is another reason why we should opt for the bundled solution – the DIY solution leaves the task of installing and configuring Nginx to us. While this is definitely not a complicated task, it does add yet another layer of work to the DIY solution. I realize this is a lot of information to take in when considering hosting options, but if you want to learn more about Nginx and related topics, please take a look at the following sites:

- `https://www.nginx.com/`
- `https://docs.nginx.com/nginx/admin-guide/installing-nginx/installing-nginx-open-source/`
- `https://unit.nginx.org/howto/rails/`

Lastly, we need to bear in mind that Rails will behave differently when run locally than in a production environment, and that includes how we view errors on a server.

Error gossip and last words

So far, we've only used the Rails framework with most of the default options. These default options include some configurations that would otherwise hinder and slow down the overall experience for the end user. These options make sense in development, as they make debugging and testing really easy. As developers, we need to be able to set up our local environment as soon as possible and start programming away. However, these default options do not make sense in a production environment. One of these defaults concerns error reporting. We saw locally how errors are displayed, but in a real-life scenario, we would never want these errors to be shown in the same way. We would not want detailed error output stating paths, variables, or even what database we're using, as this could be a security breach, or at least the beginning of one. We would want the error to be like gossip: quiet and behind our backs. And that's exactly what we're going to do. For this last exercise, we will need to load a Rails application as we've done in previous chapters. If you haven't downloaded the source code for the course, open a terminal and type the following `git` command:

```
git clone https://github.com/PacktPublishing/From-PHP-to-Ruby-on-
Rails.git
```

If you've already done so, then just navigate into the `chapter10` folder within your project by running the following command:

```
cd From-PHP-to-Ruby-on-Rails/chapter10/hosting_original/
```

Again, let's install our dependencies with the following command:

```
bundle install
```

And to confirm our setup was done correctly, let's run the following command:

```
bundle exec rails -version
```

The output should read something like the following:

```
Rails 7.0.6
```

And now we are ready to run our Rails application in production. We do this by adding the `RAILS_ENV=production` environment variable before the Rails startup command. Let's give it a try. In our shell, let's type the following:

```
RAILS_ENV=production bundle exec rails server
```

Once we run the preceding command, our application will run as usual, and our shell will look like this:

```
=> Booting Puma
=> Rails 7.0.6 application starting in production
=> Run `bin/rails server --help` for more startup options
Puma starting in single mode...
*  Puma version: 5.6.6 (ruby 3.1.1-p18) ("Birdie's Version")
*   Min threads: 5
*   Max threads: 5
*   Environment: production
*           PID: 6073
* Listening on http://0.0.0.0:3000

Use Ctrl-C to stop
```

But now, if we go to our browser and navigate to `http://0.0.0.0:3000`, we are now greeted with this page:

Figure 10.4 – Rails running in production mode

Granted, for development, this is a hassle, but trust me, you will be thankful when this page shows on your application deployed in production. As we are running our application in production mode, all errors are hidden. Now we need to look for the error in our logs. So far, we've neglected our log files, as the errors were always shown on the browser, but the logs have always been there. If we look at the `chapter10/hosting_original/log/` folder, we now have two files:

Figure 10.5 – Rails log files

Since we are running our application in production, let's open the `production.log` file. If there is too much information in the log, we can delete the contents of the file, save the file, and then refresh the browser. Now we can look at the file again with less data. We should now see something like this:

```
INFO -- : Started GET "/users/sign_in" for 127.0.0.1 at 2023-08-31
22:28:41 -0700
INFO -- : Processing by Devise::SessionsController#new as HTML
INFO -- : Completed 500 Internal Server Error in 5ms (ActiveRecord:
0.5ms | Allocations: 981)


FATAL -- :
ActiveRecord::StatementInvalid (Could not find table 'users'):
...
```

We notice the FATAL keyword, which is what caused our error. The error states that we cannot find the 'users' table. This is because we have not run the Rails migrations. So, let's do that. Let's stop our application by pressing *Ctrl + C*, and run the following command on our shell:

```
RAILS_ENV=production bundle exec rails db:migrate
```

Don't forget to prefix our command with the environment. The command should produce output detailing that the tables have been created:

```
I== 20230817050336 CreateFriends: migrating =======================
-- create_table(:friends)
   -> 0.0005s
== 20230817050336 CreateFriends: migrated (0.0005s)===============
== 20230817200425 DeviseCreateUsers: migrating ===================

-- create_table(:users)
   -> 0.0006s
-- add_index(:users, :email, {:unique=>true})
   -> 0.0001s
-- add_index(:users, :reset_password_token, {:unique=>true})
   -> 0.0001s
== 20230817200425 DeviseCreateUsers: migrated (0.0008s) ==========
```

Now let's restart our Rails application by typing the following on the shell again:

```
RAILS_ENV=production bundle exec rails server
```

Now, refresh the browser. It looks the same, with just an error page. Let's delete the contents of our production.log file again and refresh our browser once more. Now when we look at the log file again, we see a different FATAL error:

```
...

FATAL -- :
ActionView::Template::Error (The asset "application.css" is not
present in the asset pipeline.
):
...
```

I've removed the rest of the log for clarity, but the FATAL error is what gives us a clue as to the problem. In Rails, when executing our application in production, some assets need to be compiled or transpiled. In this case, it's the CSS and JavaScript assets that need to be generated and minified. Fortunately, Rails has a command to do this task. To do that, we need to stop our application with *Ctrl + C* on the shell and then run the following command:

```
RAILS_ENV=production rails assets:precompile
```

This should output a series of messages stating that the assets have been generated:

```
INFO -- : Writing hosting_original/public/assets/manifest-b84bfa46a33d
7f0dc4d2e7b8889486c9a957a5e40713d58f54be71b66954a1ff.js
INFO -- : Writing hosting_original/public/assets/manifest-b84bfa46a33d
7f0dc4d2e7b8889486c9a957a5e40713d58f54be71b66954a1ff.js.gz
INFO -- : Writing hosting_original/public/assets/application-e0cf9d8fc
b18bf7f909d8d91a5e78499f82ac29523d475bf3a9ab265d5e2b451.css
...
```

There are a lot of files that were generated, but we're not going to get into details as to how the mechanism works. Let's just say that the frontend assets were generated. Now let's run our application once more with the following command:

```
RAILS_ENV=production bundle exec rails server
```

And when we refresh the browser once more, we should see a familiar page:

Figure 10.6 – Rails login page

Congratulations, my dear readers! We are now running a Rails application in production mode. As you can see, it's a lot more hassle to debug our application as the error messages are now hidden in logs. In a real production environment, we would have to look for where these logs were kept. Running Rails tasks (db, generators, assets, etc.) might also not prove to be so straightforward. You might have to tweak the commands, and in some cases, will not be allowed to run them at all. Either way, for now, this is the end of the road and I applaud you readers for sticking with me in this Ruby-on-Rails voyage.

Summary

We covered a lot of information in this chapter. We learned about the costs of hosting, the different options on the market, and whether it makes sense to opt for a bundled solution with everything configured for us, or a DIY option, which offers more flexibility but is also more complex and expensive. We also learned why we should deploy our applications behind Nginx. Finally, we learned how to debug an application in production mode.

We are now ready to use what we've learned in this book and add Ruby to our arsenal.

Index

www.packtpub.com

Subscribe to our online digital library for full access to over 7,000 books and videos, as well as industry leading tools to help you plan your personal development and advance your career. For more information, please visit our website.

Why subscribe?

- Spend less time learning and more time coding with practical eBooks and Videos from over 4,000 industry professionals

- Improve your learning with Skill Plans built especially for you

- Get a free eBook or video every month

- Fully searchable for easy access to vital information

- Copy and paste, print, and bookmark content

Did you know that Packt offers eBook versions of every book published, with PDF and ePub files available? You can upgrade to the eBook version at packtpub.com and as a print book customer, you are entitled to a discount on the eBook copy. Get in touch with us at customercare@packtpub.com for more details.

At www.packtpub.com, you can also read a collection of free technical articles, sign up for a range of free newsletters, and receive exclusive discounts and offers on Packt books and eBooks.

Other Books You May Enjoy

If you enjoyed this book, you may be interested in these other books by Packt:

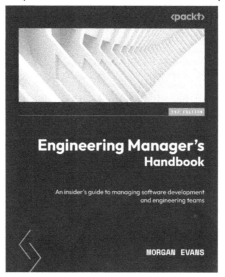

Engineering Manager's Handbook

Morgan Evans

ISBN: 978-1-80323-535-6

- Pitfalls common to new managers and how to avoid them
- Ways to establish trust and authority
- Methods and tools for building world-class engineering teams
- Behaviors to build and maintain a great reputation as a leader
- Mechanisms to avoid costly missteps that end up requiring re-work
- Strategies to increase employee retention on your team
- Techniques to facilitate better product outcomes

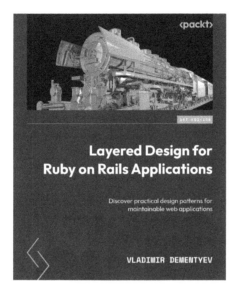

Layered Design for Ruby on Rails Applications

Vladimir Dementyev

ISBN: 978-1-80181-378-5

- Discover Rails' core components and its request/response cycle
- Understand Rails' convention-over-configuration principle and its impact on development
- Explore patterns for flexibility, extensibility, and testability in Rails
- Identify and address Rails' anti-patterns for cleaner code
- Implement design patterns for handling bloated models and messy views
- Expand from mailers to multi-channel notification deliveries
- Explore different authorization models and layers
- Use a class-based approach to configuration in Rails

Packt is searching for authors like you

If you're interested in becoming an author for Packt, please visit authors.packtpub.com and apply today. We have worked with thousands of developers and tech professionals, just like you, to help them share their insight with the global tech community. You can make a general application, apply for a specific hot topic that we are recruiting an author for, or submit your own idea.

Hi!

I am Bernard Pineda, author of *From PHP to Ruby on Rails*. I really hope you enjoyed reading this book and found it useful for increasing your productivity and efficiency using Ruby on Rails.

It would really help me (and other potential readers!) if you could leave a review on Amazon sharing your thoughts on this book.

Go to the link below or scan the QR code to leave your review:

https://packt.link/r/1804610097

Your review will help us to understand what's worked well in this book, and what could be improved upon for future editions, so it really is appreciated.

Best Wishes,

Bernard Pineda

Download a free PDF copy of this book

Thanks for purchasing this book!

Do you like to read on the go but are unable to carry your print books everywhere?

Is your eBook purchase not compatible with the device of your choice?

Don't worry, now with every Packt book you get a DRM-free PDF version of that book at no cost.

Read anywhere, any place, on any device. Search, copy, and paste code from your favorite technical books directly into your application.

The perks don't stop there, you can get exclusive access to discounts, newsletters, and great free content in your inbox daily

Follow these simple steps to get the benefits:

1. Scan the QR code or visit the link below

https://packt.link/free-ebook/9781804610091

2. Submit your proof of purchase

3. That's it! We'll send your free PDF and other benefits to your email directly

www.ingramcontent.com/pod-product-compliance
Lightning Source LLC
Chambersburg PA
CBHW080638060326
40690CB00021B/4979